Piety in Song

Spiritual Themes in Brethren Hymnody

Peter E. Roussakis

WIPF & STOCK · Eugene, Oregon

Wipf and Stock Publishers
199 W 8th Ave, Suite 3
Eugene, OR 97401

Piety in Song
Spiritual Themes in Brethren Hymnody
By Roussakis, Peter E.
Copyright©2016 Apostolos
ISBN 13: 978-1-5326-6982-8
Publication date 9/23/2018
Previously published by Apostolos, 2016

Hymns [in German piety] were written to serve as meditations, to teach individuals how to become better followers of Jesus, to reinforce sermon content, to undergird people's faith, to give succor in all manner of adverse and trying circumstances, to encourage the Christian not to give up hope but to set the goal upon heavenly things.

Hedda Durnbaugh

The spiritual life has often been described as a pilgrimage of striving to live not according to the thinking, proclivities and patterns of the world (e.g. John 17:13–19; Rom 12:1–2), but according to the Holy Spirit's influence, shaping the mind and fashioning one's character and conduct (e.g. Rom 8:1–11; Gal 6:7–10). Pilgrimage has been one of the dominant themes of Brethren spirituality.

Preface

This study is an outgrowth of this writer's lecture-presentations on Brethren hymnody given at the Fifth Brethren World Assembly held at the Brethren Heritage Center, Brookville, Ohio, July 11–14, 2013. The theme of the conference was Brethren Spirituality: How Brethren Conceive of and Practice the Spiritual Life. The lectures and seminars of the proceedings were published in 2015 by the Brethren Encyclopedia, Inc.

Christian spirituality has several aspects. The term refers to the relationship believers in Christ have with God through their faith in Jesus. It involves oneness or union with Christ made possible by his life, death, resurrection, ascension, and intercession on our behalf (Rom 6:5; 1 Cor 6:17; 1 John 4:13). In particular, Christian spirituality refers to the process of becoming more like Jesus through the enablement of his Spirit, who dwells within the center of the believer's spiritual self (Rom 8:29; Eph 5:1; Phil 2:3–13; Col 2:6–7) shaping one's inward dispositions and convictions as well as one's outer actualizations and expressions.

In Christian theological parlance, other terms which may be synonymous (at least in part) with spirituality include piety, godliness, holiness, devotion, and most certainly sanctification, which is the process of the believer's progressive transformation into the likeness of Christ (2 Cor 3:18; 1 Thess 5:23); that is, becoming more like Jesus in thought, inclination, and behavior. This transformation is made possible by God's Spirit through the individual's intentional, sincere, and voluntary submission to the Christian pattern of life, and may be cultivated through engagement in such formative means of God's grace as: worshiping; singing psalms, hymns and songs; learning the teachings of the sacred writings; prayer and contemplation; partaking of the sacraments; fasting; and service to others.

Because sanctification is a life-long process, the spiritual life has often been described as a pilgrimage, with the pilgrim striving to live not according to the thinking, proclivities, and patterns of the world (John 17:13–19; Rom 12:1–2), but according to the Holy Spirit, allowing the Spirit's influence to shape and fashion one's character, mind, and conduct (Rom 8:1–11; Gal 6:7–10). Indeed, the idea of pilgrimage has been one of the dominant themes of Brethren spirituality.

The Brethren of whom we are speaking observed their 300th anniversary in 2008. In the nineteenth century they called themselves The Fraternity of German Baptists and the German Baptist Brethren. Their beginnings in 1708 were in the little village of Schwarzenau, Germany, under the leadership of Alexander Mack Sr. (1679–1735). Due to religious persecution, most of these Brethren had emigrated to America by the 1730s. By the 1880s the Brethren were divided over several issues: notably whether or not they should be engaged in higher education, have Sunday schools, participate in evangelistic endeavors and foreign missions, and use musical instruments in worship. The controversies led to schism and the formation of three distinct groups: the more cautious, conservative parent remained the largest of these bodies and retained the name German Baptist Brethren. The other two were a progressive group called The Brethren Church, and the ultra-conservatives known as the Old German Baptist Brethren. Today, there are several main groups which share this common heritage: the German Baptist Brethren (who were renamed the Church of the Brethren in 1908), The Brethren Church, The Fellowship of Grace Brethren Churches, the Conservative Grace Brethren Churches International; the Old German Baptist Brethren, the Old German Baptist Brethren New Conference, and the Dunkard Brethren Church.

This volume highlights the spiritual themes of the Brethren as illuminated in their hymnody from their beginnings through the three hundred years to 2008. Some of the areas to be examined include: the thinking and influences which shaped what hymns Brethren chose to sing; the themes of which the Brethren authors wrote; which hymns Brethren hymnal compilers and committees chose to include; which tunes the Brethren chose to accompany their hymns; why Brethren musicians composed the tunes as they did; and the manner in which the Brethren rendered their singing. Included, therefore, is a discussion of the major Brethren hymn book publications, hymn text writers and translators, hymn tune composers, and worship and singing practices. Specific attention is given to examples of hymn texts which highlight the distinctive themes and characteristics of Brethren spirituality in the various eras of Brethren life and thought.

For the period 1900–2008, the discussion will focus primarily on the hymnody of the Church of the Brethren, for this was the only Brethren group to produce new hymnals during this period. I sincerely regret that it would be impossible in a work of this size to highlight all of the many fine authors and composers who have blessed the Brethren church with their words and tunes. The intention here has been not to present a comprehensive overview of Brethren hymnody, but rather to discuss and highlight the distinctive spiritual themes of the Brethren as expressed in their hymnody through the rich and most interesting history of the first 300 years of the Brethren movement.

P.E.R., Spring 2016

Contents

Introduction 11

Emerging: Pre-1708–Early 19th Century 18

Suffering Pilgrim 18

Geistreiches Gesang-Buch (1720) 19

Alexander Mack Sr. (1679–1735) 23

Wilhelm Knepper (1691–c. 1743) 25

Undocumented Hymns in *Geistreiches Gesang-Buch* (1720) 26

Emigration 27

Das Kleine Davidische Psalterspiel der Kinder Zions (1744) 29

Alexander Mack Jr. (1712–1803) 31

Worship 35

Die Kleine Harfe (1792) 36

Peter Becker (1687–1758) 37

Jakob Danner (1727–c.1800) 37

Alexander Mack Jr. (1712–1803) 38

Christopher Sauer Jr. (1721–1784) 39

Johannes Naas (1669–1741) 40

Jakob Stoll (1731–1822) and the End of an Era 43

Expanding: Late 18th Century to Mid-19th Century 48

The Christian's Duty (1791) 49

Die Kleine Lieder Sammlung (1826) 54

A Choice Selection of Hymns (1830) 57

Die Kleine Perlen-Sammlung (1858) 57

Nineteenth Century Brethren Spirituality, Worship and Music Practices 61

Excepting: Mid-19th Century to the 1880s 67

A Collection of Psalms, Hymns, and Spiritual Songs (1867) Neue Sammlung (1870) 68

Das Christliche Gesang-Buch (1874) Ein Sammlung von Psalmen, Lobesängen, und Geistlichen Liedern (1893) 72

The Brethren's Tune and Hymn Book (1872, 1879) John Cook Ewing (1849–1937) 74

A Collection of Hymns and Sacred Songs (1882) 78

Energizing: The 1880s to Early 20th Century 81

The Brethren Hymnody with Tunes (1884) John Cook Ewing (1849–1937) 81

The Brethren's Sunday School Song Book (1894) William Beery (1852–1956) and Other Composers 88

The Brethren Hymnal (1901) 92

Evolving: Early 20th Century to 1958 100

Hymnal: Church of the Brethren (1925) 101

James Montgomery (1771–1854) 104

Broad Spectrum of Inclusions: Evolving Spirituality 108

The Brethren Hymnal (1951) 115

Anniversary Hymns (1958) 122

End of an Era 122

Endeavoring: Later 20th Century to 2008 125

The Brethren Songbook (1974, 1979) 125

Developments 126

Hymnal: A Worship Book (1992) and Hymnal Companion (1996); Hymnal Supplement (2001 & Periodically Onward) 127

German Baptist Brethren Youth Sing................................134

End of Another Era 134

Postscript 137

Index (With Selected Hymn Texts, Tunes, Authors and Composers)..138

Introduction

It was Albert T. Ronk (1886–1972) in his *History of The Brethren Church* who remarked: "A strong German characteristic is the possession of an inherent musical sense."[1] The Brethren from their beginnings sang, and they have been singing ever since, because they have grasped the ability of singing hymns to connect them with spiritual reality. Indeed, their hymn singing is one of the outward expressions of the inward convictions of their spirituality.

German hymnody from Martin Luther (1483–1546) onward restored parishioner participation in worship through congregational singing. Theirs was a rich tradition, whether Lutheran or Reformed, which boasted a wealth of texts and chorale tunes. It is from this "stock" of German hymnody that the early Brethren drew for their own first hymn books. Perhaps without fully understanding or articulating it, German Brethren apprehended the capacity of music to mirror the rhythms of human emotions, meaning that for them music played a naturally prominent role in everyday life in general, and especially in the worship of God.[2]

---

[1] Albert T. Ronk. *History of the Brethren Church: Its Life, Thought, Mission* (Ashland, OH: Brethren Publishing Company, 1968), 65.

[2] The capacity of music to mirror the rhythms of our emotions was explained by Suzanne K. Langer (1895–1985), professor of philosophy at Radcliff, Smith, and Wellesley Colleges, Connecticut College for Women, and Columbia University, in *Feeling and Form* (New York: Charles Scribner's Sons, 1952), 27–29. "The tonal structures we call music bear a close logical similarity to the forms of human feeling, forms of growth and of attenuation, flowing and stowing, conflict and resolutions, speed, arrest, terrific excitement, calm or subtle activation and dreamy lapses ... the greatness and brevity and eternal passing of everything virtually felt.... Music is a tonal analogue of emotive life ... music has import, and this import is the pattern of sentience, the pattern of life itself, as it is felt and directly known."

Music, as an art form, speaks to the total person—the senses as well as the intellect—and this is especially true of word-based musical pieces (such as in hymns). The scriptures attest to this truth. Paul wrote: "I will sing praise with the spirit, but I will sing with the mind also" (1 Cor 14:15 *NRSV*). When combined with words, the ingredients of music serve to capture the sense and the mood of the ideas expressed in those words, to emotively shape, enliven, heighten, enhance, and impress the ideas the words conveyed to the minds and hearts of those who heard and sang them.[3]

Brethren have understood that hymn singing not only enables the believer to praise God, give thanks and pray (Ps 95:1–2) but that it also provides a vehicle for poetically proclaiming the revelation of God (1 Chron 25:1), for teaching the truths of the faith (Col 3:16), and for strengthening and edifying the faithful during all the experiences of life's journey (1 Cor 14:26). James Quinter (1816–1888), in the Preface of the 1867 hymnbook published by him for the Brethren, echoed these thoughts and the famous remark by Martin Luther that next to the Word of God music deserves the highest praise.[4] Quinter wrote: "Singing

---

[3] The question may be raised by the non-musician regarding *how* music, particularly hymn singing, relates to us and mirrors the emotive rhythms we experience. Using general terminology, it does so through the variety of ways that the *ingredients* of music are fashioned and performed in each piece. Music consists of *sounds* which can be higher or lower in *pitch*, longer or shorter in *duration*, louder or softer in *volume* (dynamics). Tones can be grouped together in *pulses* of three counts, four counts, or any other grouping a composer chooses, otherwise known as *meter*. *Melodies* and *harmonies* have a *rhythm* (the combination of the longer and shorter durations of pitches) of their own which shapes the textual/musical ideas expressed. All of the above may be rendered in a faster or slower speed, or *tempo*. Greater treatment of this subject is given in Peter E. Roussakis' *Classic Worship: With Brethren in Mind* (Burlington, IN: Meetinghouse Press, 2005), 79–95.

[4] Luther said: "We are able to adduce only this one point at present, namely, that experience proves that, next to the Word of God, only music deserves being

the praises of God may justly be regarded as an important part of the worship we offer to him.... The relation that the Hymn Book stands in to singing in the Church is such, that gives it a place next in importance to the Bible, among Christians ... the Hymn Book is an important auxiliary in promoting Christian worship and edification."[5]

Dennis D. Martin in his "Devotional Literature" entry in *The Brethren Encyclopedia* explained: "During the 18th and 19th centuries Brethren devotional literature consisted primarily of the Bible and the countless poems and hymns.... More hymnals were published between 1790 and 1845 than any other form of literary expression."[6]

Moreover, when Brethren sing together, fellowship is cultivated, as oneness and cohesiveness are enhanced. To use the words of Karl Barth (1886–1968): "The Christian community sings.... Its singing is not a concert. But from inner, material necessity, it sings. Singing is the highest form of expression ... [and] the community which does not sing is not the community."[7]

We have at our disposal, therefore, hymns and hymnbooks—and later hymn and tune books—as a significant source and expression of how Brethren conceived of and practiced the

---

extolled as the mistress and governess of the feelings of the human heart ... the Fathers and Prophets desired not in vain that nothing be more intimately linked up with the Word of God than music." Cited in Walter E. Buszin, "Luther on Music," *The Musical Quarterly*, Vol. 22 (1946), 81.

[5] *A Collection of Psalms, Hymns and Spiritual Songs; suited to the various kinds of Christian Worship; and especially designed for, and adapted to, the Fraternity of the Brethren.* Compiled by direction of the Annual Meeting, upon the basis of the Hymn Books formerly used by the Brotherhood (Covington, OH: James Quinter, 1867), iii.

[6] Dennis D. Martin, "Devotional Literature," *The Brethren Encyclopedia*, Vol. 1 (Philadelphia, PA; Oakbrook, IL: The Brethren Encyclopedia, Inc., 1983), 381.

[7] Karl Barth, *Church Dogmatics* Vol. 4.3 (Edinburgh: T&T Clark, 1962), 866–867.

spiritual life. In particular, we shall be citing some of the persons, writings, events, and experiences which influenced the Brethren in the shaping of the content of their hymnic expressions and their singing practices.

An over-arching theme which may be traced throughout Brethren history and hymnody has been discussed by Dennis D. Martin in his "Spiritual Life" entry.

> The prevailing interpretation of the history of Brethren spiritual life focuses on a supposed dialectic tension between inwardness and obedience (fruit-bearing). Scholars have identified inner devotion with the radical Pietist tradition and have linked the desire to be obedient to the letter of the New Testament commandments to the Anabaptist heritage of the Brethren ... the earliest Brethren sought to affirm both inward fervor and outward obedience (discipleship) while Brethren in the 19th century were preoccupied with outward expressions of their Brethren identity.[8]

In his work, *The First Love of the Community of Jesus Christ, that is: True Portrayal* [Abbildung] *of the First Christians* (1696), Gottfried Arnold (1666–1714)—the Radical Pietist theologian and devotional writer whose thought greatly influenced the early Brethren—discussed true worship as a combination of commitment of the self to God as a living sacrifice (Rom 12:1) and the practice of good works (James 1:27).[9] Regarding music, Arnold (a hymn-writer himself) affirmed that the early church practiced singing hymns as a

---

[8] Dennis D. Martin, "Spiritual Life," *The Brethren Encyclopedia,* Vol. 2 (Philadelphia, PA; Oakbrook, IL: The Brethren Encyclopedia Inc., 1983), 1209.

[9] Dale R. Stoffer, *Background and Development of Brethren Doctrines 1650–1987* (Philadelphia, PA: The Brethren Encyclopedia, Inc., 1989), 32, regarding the thought in Arnold's *Die Erste Liebe Der Gemeinen Jesu Christi, Das ist: Wahre Abbildung Der Ersten Christen.*

congregational act of worship. He emphasized, however, that they rendered their singing in a *plain* manner, meaning unaccompanied and in unison; a practice which remained among many Brethren through much of the nineteenth century, and among the Old German Baptist Brethren to this day.[10] In Arnold's view, singing along with praying and the exposition of the written Word were important expressions of the early church's spirituality. He cautioned, however, that a corresponding inward devotion must accompany each outward exercise (e.g. Eph 5:19; 1 Cor 14:26).[11]

Stanza one of Arnold's hymn, "The Kingdom of God," is given here as translated by Catherine Winkworth (1827–1878).

> *Anoint us with Thy blessed love*
> *O Wisdom, through and through,*
> *Till Thy sweet impulses remove*
> *All dread and fear undue,*
> *And we behold ourselves in Thee*
> *A purified Humanity,*
> *And live Thy risen life.*[12]

Thoughts similar to Arnold's regarding adhering to the principles and practices of primitive Christianity were expressed in the nineteenth century by Brethren Elder Peter Nead (1796–1877) in his theological writings. He said that while there is a "great deal of singing done which I believe is an abomination unto God," nevertheless, "singing, if performed agreeably to the Word and Spirit of God, is a part of that holy devotion in

---

[10] Discussed in Hedwig T. Durnbaugh's "Music in Worship, 1708–1850," *Brethren Life and Thought* (Volume XXXIII, Autumn 1988, Number Four), 271.

[11] Stoffer, *Brethren Doctrines*, 33.

[12] Catherine Winkworth, *Christian Singers of Germany* (New York: MacMillan, 1869), 293–294.

worshipping the true and living God."[13] His caution, therefore, resulted in singing hymns *slowly* so that all would focus on the meaning of the hymn texts.[14]

Colonial Brethren Elder Michael Frantz (1687–1748) was also a writer of poetry and prose, some of each contained within his *Simple Doctrinal-Considerations*, published posthumously by Christopher Sauer Jr. (1721–1784) in 1770. This brief yet comprehensive presentation of seventy pages is the most thorough summary of Brethren belief in the colonial era. In one of the prose articles, *Of Inner Communion with God*, Frantz wrote: "If the inward communion with God has been truly realized, it will issue in outward communion ... with all kinds of virtues of love.... To love one's neighbor as one's self shows clearly what communion is."[15]

During the span of Brethren history, their hymnody reflected their major beliefs and practices. At other times they mirrored a melding of their distinctives with emphases in the greater Christian community. Even though over time the particular kinds of literary expression of Brethren thought, and the hymn tune repertoire (originally sung in their German hymnody) were abandoned, many of the themes which were present in the eighteenth century are found in the English language hymn books of the Brethren in the nineteenth century in one form or another.

---

[13] Peter Nead. *Theological Writings on Various Subjects; or a Vindication of Primitive Christianity* (Dayton, OH: New Edition, 1866; repr. Dunker Springhaus Ministries, Youngstown, OH, 1997), 176–177.

[14] Ibid., 176.

[15] Cited in Donald F. Durnbaugh, *Fruit of the Vine: A History of the Brethren 1708–1995* (Elgin, IL: Brethren Press, 1997), 138. The full title of Frantz's work is *Einfältige Lehr-Betraehtungen, und Kurtzgefasztes, Glaubens-Bekäntinsz des Lebens, Michael Frantzen* (Simple Doctrinal Considerations and a Concise Confession of Faith of the Pious Teacher, Michael Frantz). See also Stoffer, *Brethren Doctrines*, 96–97 for treatment of this subject.

The chapters of the present volume are organized according to several historical characterizations, each with examples of hymns which highlight significant spiritual themes. The divisions are the following:

Emerging: (Pre-1708 to Early 19th Century)

Expanding: (Late 18th Century to Mid-19th Century)

Excepting: (Mid-19th Century to the 1880s)

Energizing: (1880s to Early 20th Century)

Evolving: (Early 20th Century to 1958)

Endeavoring: (Later 20th Century to 2008)

Emerging: Pre-1708–Early 19th Century

Why do we view the length of this period as one division? The commonness of thought which the Brethren expressed in their worshiping practices and literary output leads us to consider the whole of the eighteenth century as the Emerging era of Brethren spirituality and hymnic activity. Again, citing Dennis D. Martin's summary in his "Spiritual Life" entry in *The Brethren Encyclopedia*: "Church discipline, a fervent desire to recover primitive Christianity and the desire to grow in humility through literal observance of the ordinances described in the New Testament ... formed Brethren spirituality in the first generation. Worship was not a time for exaltation but for humbling."[16] Hymn singing played a prominent role in early Brethren worship, along with praying and the reading and interpretation of Scripture. Patterned after a typical Radical Pietist worship meeting, early Brethren house worship was described as follows:

> When they come together they sing two or three hymns, as God moves them; then they open the Bible and whatever they find they read and explain it according to the understanding given to them by God, for the edification of their brethren. After they have read, they fall to their knees, raise their hands to God, and pray for their authorities that God might move them to punish the evil and protect the good. Then they praise God that He has created them for this purpose.[17]

Suffering Pilgrim

This description of early Brethren worship (singing, reading, explaining, praying, praising) was given following the arrest of

---

[16] Martin, "Spiritual Life," *The Brethren Encyclopedia*, 1209.

[17] Donald F. Durnbaugh, *Fruit of the Vine*, 20–21.

several Brethren for holding illegal Pietist house meetings. It is not surprising, therefore, that the "chief metaphor for the spiritual life among the Brethren from Alexander Mack Sr. to Jacob Stoll (d. 1822) was the life of a suffering pilgrim in a sinful world."[18] Moreover, it was John Samuel Flory (1866–1961) who remarked that the death in 1803 of Alexander Mack Jr., considered the most literary of all Brethren in this era, "marks the passage of the first group of great men who lent lustre to the early history of the church, and who produced the first important body of our church literature."[19]

Other prominent themes in the devotional literature, including the hymns of the colonial period, were the "cultivation of loving communion with God, the denial of self and the world, perseverance in the Christian life, faithful discipleship to Christ, eternal salvation and judgment, and frequent reference to Christ's life and work."[20]

Geistreiches Gesang-Buch (1720)

Not only are we able to cite influences for hymn content and singing practices, but also for the compilation and arrangement of hymn books. The first Brethren hymnal, *Geistreiches Gesang-Buch (Spirit-filled Hymn-Book)*, published by Christoph Konert at Berleburg in 1720, included hymns with distinct Brethren themes, baptism by immersion and foot-washing for example. The hymn book had as its chief sources, two Pietist hymn books: *Geistreiches Gesang-Buch* published in two installments (1704, 1714) at Halle by Johann Anastasius Freylinghausen (1670–1739), son-in-law of the Pietist leader August Hermann Francke (1663–1727), and which became the standard

---

[18] Martin, "Spiritual Life," *The Brethren Encyclopedia,* 1209.
[19] J. S. Flory, *Literary Activity of the German Baptist Brethren in the Eighteenth Century* (Elgin, IL: Brethren Publishing House, 1908), ix.
[20] Stoffer, *Brethren Doctrines*, 89.

hymnbook of the Pietist movement, including the early Brethren; and *Davidische Psalterspiel der Kinder Zions (Davidic Psaltery of the Children of Zion)* published by the Radical Pietist Community of True Inspiration in 1718. 157 of the 295 hymns in the 1720 hymnal appeared in the Freylinghausen and Inspirationist hymn books.[21]

Identifying the sources tells us what kinds of hymns and tunes would have been sung by the early Brethren prior to the publication of *Geistreiches Gesang-Buch* 1720.[22] In the 1720 hymn book there are entries which represent the span of the German Chorale heritage,[23] including Martin Luther's early

---

[21] While the 1720 hymn book did not have a topical index, a listing of what could have been the rubrics of the hymn book is given in Hedwig T. Durnbaugh's *The German Hymnody of the Brethren 1720–1903* (Philadelphia, PA: The Brethren Encyclopedia, Inc., 1986), 142–143.

[22] A complete listing of the hymn-writers represented in the 1720 hymn book is given in Hedda Durnbaugh, *The German Hymnody of the Brethren 1720–1903*, 38–39, and in Appendix IX, an Index of First Lines.

[23] Leading up to the 1720 hymn book were several periods of German hymnody. The Early Reformation Era (c.1517–1577) is represented by hymns of Martin Luther. Sources of chorale melodies in this period included Gregorian Chant, Leisen (pre-Reformation folk hymns), Contrafaction (a sacred text wedded to an already popular secular melody), Cantios (Latin spiritual songs of pre-Reformation times which, although religious in content, were not associated directly with the liturgy), and newly-composed hymns. The term *chorale* originally reflected its origin in the German word "choral" meaning the Gregorian chant source. The term came to be known as referring to the variety of roots and origins. Discussion is given by Carl F. Schalk, "German Hymnody," *Hymnal Companion to the Lutheran Book of Worship* by Marilyn Kay Stulken (Philadelphia: Fortress, 1981), 19–23.

One representative hymn writer of the Period of Lutheran Orthodoxy (c.1577–1617) is Philipp Nicolai (1556–1608), his most well-known hymns being *Wachet auf, ruft uns die Stimme (Wake, awake, for night is flying)* and *Wie schön leuchet der Morgenstern (O morning star, how fair and bright)* for which Nicolai wrote both the texts and tunes.

chorale of 1524, *Nun Bitten wir den Heiligen Geist (Now let us Pray to the Holy Ghost)*. Hymns in this period were sung in unison by the congregation and originally without accompaniment.[24]

The hymns and tunes of Philipp Nicolai (1556–1608) marked the beginning of a transition from more objective and confessional

---

The first two-thirds of the 17th century included the Thirty Years' War (1618–1648) and a revival in the writing of hymns. The great distress of the war was a significant factor in the transition to more subjectivity in hymns being realized. "It was inevitable that the hymnody which developed in this period increasingly sought to relate more closely to the life situations in which the people found themselves." (Schalk, *Hymnal Companion*, 26). Examples include those of two Lutheran pastors, Martin Rinkart's (1568–1649) *Nun danket alle Gott (Now thank we all our God)*, and Paul Gerhardt's (1607–1676) *O Haupt voll Blut und wunden (O sacred Head, sore wounded)*; and by lawyer Johann Franck (1618–1677) with his *Jesu meine Freude (Jesus, priceless treasure)*. Gerhardt's organist-composer colleague at St. Nicholas Church in Berlin, Johann Crüger (1598–1662), composed many chorale tunes, such as NUN DANKET (for *Now thank we all our God*), and JESU, MEINE FREUDE (for *Jesus, priceless treasure*). Crüger's chorale tune collection, *Praxis pietatis melica (Practice of Piety in Song)* of 1644 was the most significant Lutheran hymn book of that century.

The Period of Pietism in German hymnody is the context for the production of the Freylinghausen and Inspirationist hymn books, which became the primary sources of many of the hymns in the 1720 hymn book. "The effect of Pietism on the texts written during these times was to place an even greater emphasis on the personal subjective aspects of the Christian life. Individualistic, privatistic, and even mystical aspects of religion received even greater stress in hymn texts often intended for private devotional use but which increasingly found their way into hymnals to be used in corporate worship" (Schalk, *Hymnal Companion*, 29). Of particular note are German Reformed hymnists Joachim Neander (1650–1680) who wrote *Lobe den Herren den mächtgen (Praise to the Lord, the Almighty)*, and Gerhard Tersteegen (1697–1769), author of *Gott is gegenwärtig (God Himself is present)*.

[24] Manfred F. Bukofzer, *Music in the Baroque Era* (New York: W. W. Norton & Company, Inc., 1947), 79.

hymnody to hymns with a more personal devotional character.[25] Included in this first Brethren hymn book is his *Wachet auf, Ruft uns die Stimme* (*Wake, Awake, for Night is Flying*, WACHET AUF), often referred to as the "King of Chorales."

The great distress of the Thirty Years' War (1618–1648) was a significant factor in the transition to more subjectivity in hymns being realized. Examples in *Geistreiches Gesang-Buch* 1720 include *Halleluja, Lob, Preis und Her'* (*Hallelujah, Thanks and Praise*) by Lutheran pastor and cantor Martin Rinkart (1568–1649); and *Folget Mir, Ruft uns das Leben* (one translation being *Follow Me, in Me ye Live*) by Lutheran minister Johann Rist (1607–1667).

Also included in the 1720 hymn book were *Befiehl du deine Wege (Give to the Winds your Fears)* and *O Jesu Christ, Mein Schonstes Licht (Jesus, thy Boundless Love to Me)* by Paul Gerhardt (1607–1676), viewed generally, next to Luther, as the greatest German hymnist, and a favorite hymn writer of the Brethren; *Jesu, Meine Freude (Jesus, Priceless Treasure)* by lawyer Johann Franck (1618–1677); *Lobe den Herren dem Mächtigen König der Ehren (Praise to the Lord, the Almighty)* by Reformed Pietist pastor Joachim Neander (1650–1680); and *Gott is Gegenwärtig (God Himself is Present)* by Gerhard Tersteegen (1697–1769), described by the German musicologist, Friedrich Blume (1893–1975), as "the only truly great poet of this period."[26]

Paul Gerhardt's organist-composer colleague at St. Nicholas Church in Berlin, Johann Crüger (1598–1662), composed many chorale tunes, such as NUN DANKET (for *Now Thank we all our God*), and JESU, MEINE FREUDE (for *Jesus, Priceless*

---

[25] Carl F. Schalk, "German Hymnody," in Marilyn Kay Stulken, ed., *Hymnal Companion to the Lutheran Book of Worship* (Philadelphia: Fortress, 1981), 25.
[26] Friedrich Blume, *Protestant Church Music: A History* (London: Victor Gollancz Ltd., 1975), 259.

Treasure). Crüger's chorale tune collection, *Praxis Pietatis Melica (Practice of Piety in Song)* of 1644 was the most significant Lutheran hymn book of that century. The title of Crüger's volume aptly describes this present work on the spiritual themes of Brethren hymnody.

Hedda Durnbaugh offered the following description of the significance of hymns in German piety: "Hymns were written to serve as meditations, to teach individuals how to become better followers of Jesus, to reinforce sermon content, to undergird people's faith, to give succor in all manner of adverse and trying circumstances, to encourage the Christian not to give up hope but to set the goal upon heavenly things."[27]

Alexander Mack Sr. (1679–1735)

Two known Brethren hymn-writers are represented in the 1720 hymn book, the first being Brethren patriarch Alexander Mack Sr., a miller by trade from Schriesheim. In addition to being influenced by the thought of Gottfried Arnold, Mack was influenced by another Radical Pietist, Ernst Christoph Hochmann von Hochenau (1670–1721), with whom Mack traveled some on evangelistic endeavors. When consulted regarding whether or not the Brethren should follow through on their conviction of baptism by immersion, also illegal, Hochmann cited Luke 14:28 about *counting the cost* regarding inevitable persecution which may follow.[28] Mack and seven others made the decision to act upon their conviction. In the summer of 1708 they prepared themselves to be baptized by immersion in Schwarzenau's Eder River by fasting, praying, singing and prayerfully reading God's written Word.[29]

---

[27] H. T. Durnbaugh, *The German Hymnody of the Brethren*, 18.

[28] Stoffer, *Brethren Doctrines*, 66–67.

[29] H. R. Holsinger, *Holsinger's History of the Tunkers and The Brethren Church* (Oakland, CA: Pacific Press Publishing Co., 1901), 36.

Alexander Mack's *Überschlag die Kost (Count the Cost)*, a teaching hymn in thirteen stanzas, is said to have been sung at baptismal services[30] and is well-known to Brethren. With this hymn we begin to see prominent themes of Brethren spirituality in their hymnody of the period. Stanzas one and two of Mack's hymn are given below, as translated by Ora W. Garber (1903–1981).

> *Christ Jesus says, "Count well the cost*
> *When you lay the foundation,*
> *Are you resolved, though all seem lost,*
> *To risk your reputation,*
> *Your self, your wealth, for Christ the Lord*
> *As you now give your solemn word?*
>
> *Into Christ's death you're buried now*
> *Through baptism's joyous union.*
> *No claim of self dare you allow*
> *If you desire communion*
> *With Christ's true church, His willing bride,*
> *Which, through His Word, He has supplied.*[31]

---

[30] William R. Eberly, ed., *The Complete Writings of Alexander Mack* (Winona Lake, IN: BMH Books, 1991), 107.

[31] This poetic rendering, authored by Ora W. Garber (1903–1981), is given in Donald F. Durnbaugh's *European Origins of the Brethren* (Elgin, IL: The Brethren Press, 1958), 408–411. A prose translation is offered by Hedwig T. Durnbaugh in her *German Hymnody of the Brethren 1720–1903*, 20–21. A chorale setting of the Garber rendering appeared in a small pamphlet, *Anniversary Hymns*, produced for the 250th anniversary of the Brethren; and in *Hymnal: A Worship Book* (Elgin, IL: Brethren Press; Newton, KS: Faith and Life Press; and Scottdale, PA: Mennonite Publishing House, 1992), hymn 437. An adapted version of the text was made by Peter E. Roussakis, wedded to the tune HENDON, and sung at the 300th Anniversary convention of the Brethren in 2008 in Richmond, Virginia. It is included at the close of the present volume.

Another example of Brethren singing at baptismal services occurred in August 1711. Beyond Schwarzenau the Brethren expanded in the Marienborn area (northeast of Frankfurt). Mack came and baptized the daughter of Eva Elizabeth Hoffman in the Seeme Brook. Following the baptism (which in the Brethren tradition is by trine immersion, one immersion for each member of the Godhead), those who had gathered, sang the last stanza of *Herr Jesu Christ, Dich zu uns Wend (Lord Jesus Christ, Turn Toward Us)* by Wilhelm II of Sachsen-Weimar.[32]

Wilhelm Knepper (1691–c. 1743)

The other known Brethren hymn-writer represented in the 1720 hymn book is Wilhelm Knepper. He was one of six men from the town of Solingen who were arrested February 1, 1717 for being baptized by immersion and holding private meetings for worship, also called conventicles. One of the six, William Grahe (1693–1763), described their experience:

> We were bound two by two around our arms.... We were thus led away to Düsseldorf, which journey we passed mostly in singing. As we were led away, we were all overwhelmed with mercy that we might now endure something for His pure truth. We sang the hymn: "O Jesus, My Bridegroom, How Happy I feel!" ["*O Jesu, mein Brautigam, wie ist mir so wohl!*"]. The excitement among the people was also very great; yes, there were many so awakened and impressed by the matter.... We prisoners were accompanied by shouts of rejoicing and went to Düsseldorf, singing most of the way.[33]

---

[32] Donald F. Durnbaugh, *European Origins of the Brethren*, 160–161; and Hedwig T. Durnbaugh's *The German Hymnody of the Brethren*, 188.

[33] Donald F. Durnbaugh, *European Origins*, 241–243. The hymn they sang was one by Ahasverus Fritzsch (1629–1701), listed in H. Durnbaugh, *German Hymnody of the Brethren*, 288.

In December 1717 they were moved to the fortress of Jülich where they were sentenced to hard labor and suffered greatly. They were released in November 1720.[34]

During their captivity, Knepper wrote some four hundred hymns. Attributed to him in the *Geistreiches Gesang-Buch* 1720 are nearly 100 of those hymns. Documented as his is *Ach wie Solieblich und wie Fein (How Pleasant is It)*, a hymn on the significance of feet-washing. The eleven stanzas were translated by Ora W. Garber. Stanza one reads:

> *How pleasant is it and how good*
> *That those who live as brothers should,*
> *In faith and love uniting,*
> *Like servants wash each other's feet,*
> *When at the feast of love they meet,*
> *In fellowship delighting.*[35]

Undocumented Hymns in *Geistreiches Gesang-Buch* (1720)

One of the undocumented hymns echoes several of the spiritual themes mentioned above.

> *Thou art a pilgrim true and tried,*
> *If self from self thou sever,*
> *And see the mind and will have died*
> *And are subdued forever.*[36]

---

[34] A full account of the Solingen Brethren's arrest and incarcerations is given in Donald F. Durnbaugh, *Fruit of the Vine*, 54–59.

[35] Included in D. Durnbaugh's *European Origins*, 415–418; and as hymn 451 in *Hymnal: A Worship Book* (1992).

[36] The hymn text, "The Christian Pilgrim," was translated by Ralph W. Schlosser (1886–1878) and is included in D. Durnbaugh's *European Origins*, 411–413.

Another undocumented hymn, although believed to be authored by Wilhelm Knepper, is worthy of mention because of its inclusion in all subsequent German hymn books of the Brethren. *Ihr Jungen Helden, Aufgewacht!* (*Awake, Ye Young Heroes*), is a hymn speaking about denial of the world. Hedda Durnbaugh's prose translation of stanza three reads: "To cease loving the world to embrace Jesus is the way to receive the power of the Spirit so that one may soon punish [the world's] actions."[37]

Terms and phrases from several hymns in the hymn book paint a negative picture of the Brethren view of the individual (e.g. stranger, useless servant, miserable worm, a withered tree barely alive) and express the position Brethren held regarding the state of humanity and the need for reconciliation through faith in and allegiance to Christ.

Emigration

Religious persecution continued to shape the early Brethren geographically. From Schwarzenau they went to the Marienborn area. Following their expulsion from there they went to Krefeld in 1715. Johannes Naas (1669–1741) was the leader of the Brethren in Krefeld, assisted by Peter Becker (1687–1758), Christian Liebe (1679–1757), and Stephen Koch (d. 1763). Becker was called upon to lead the first migration of Brethren in 1719 to America. At one point during a furious storm on their arduous ocean voyage, the Brethren maintained calm and were praying and singing, as the captain observed.[38]

The Brethren arrived in Philadelphia in the fall of 1719. The majority settled in nearby Germantown. No formal worship services were held initially. However, in the fall of 1722, Peter Becker and two others were urged to make house-to-house visits of all the Brethren who had traveled together to America in an

---

[37] Hedwig T. Durnbaugh, *German Hymnody of the Brethren*, 26.
[38] H. R. Holsinger, *History of the Tunkers and The Brethren Church*, 123–124.

attempt to unify them all and assess their interest in meeting together for worship. The canvassing bore much fruit, and they began meeting regularly in the homes of Peter Becker and Johann Gumre (d. 1738). The first baptismal service was held on Christmas Day 1723. At the Wissahickon River, following the reading of the Luke 14 passage, and the singing of Alexander Mack's hymn, "Count the cost," Peter Becker, who had been selected as elder, baptized by trine immersion several persons from the Schuylkill Valley. In the evening they gathered at the home of Johann Gumre to celebrate the Love Feast. The Love Feast is the Brethren service of Communion, which includes several elements: a time of examination, feet-washing, the Lord's Supper (which traditionally has been observed with a small meal), followed by the Eucharistic bread and cup, and hymn singing.[39]

A second major migration from Europe of about thirty families took place in 1729 under the leadership of Alexander Mack Sr. Holsinger recorded that the Germantown congregation held regular services on Sunday in the house of the printer Christopher Sauer Sr. (1695–1758). The congregation also held a weekly council meeting on Thursdays, and a Sunday afternoon meeting for unmarried members.[40] Although Sauer did not formally affiliate with the Brethren, he was supportive of them. His son, Christopher Sauer Jr., became a member in 1737. The Brethren in America continued to increase, and with that came the need for a hymnal.

---

[39] Descriptions of the day's proceedings are given, for example, in Donald F. Durnbaugh, ed., *The Brethren in Colonial America* (Elgin, IL: The Brethren Press, 1967), 61–63; and in Homer A. Kent Sr., *Conquering Frontiers: A History of the Brethren Church* (Winona Lake, IN: BMH Books, 1958), 39–45.

[40] Holsinger, *History of the Tunkers and The Brethren Church*, 179.

Das Kleine Davidische Psalterspiel der Kinder Zions (1744)

The second hymnal produced by the Brethren was published by Christopher Sauer Sr. in 1744 in Germantown, Pennsylvania. Alexander Mack, Peter Becker, and Sauer collaborated in the decision-making for this production. The hymnal was drawn from and patterned after the 1718 Inspirationist hymn book, but abridged in its number of hymns. Whereas the 1718 hymnal contained 1050 hymns, *Das Kleine Davidische Psalterspiel der Kinder Zions (The Small Davidic Psaltery of the Children of Zion)* included 536. Of the documented hymns there were 291 from the stock of German hymnody introduced to the Brethren for the first time. Of the 128 different hymn-writers represented, fifty-one were newly added. Included were thirty-one hymns by Gottfried Arnold. The thirty-two hymns by Joachim Neander, twenty-eight from the pen of Johann Schleffer (1624–1677), and twelve by Paul Gerhardt represented some of the hymn-writers favored by the Brethren. Fifty-six of the hymns attributed to Wilhelm Knepper were carried over from *Geistreiches Gesang-Buch* 1720. Also introduced were a few psalms of David metricized, which were German translations of *Genevan Psalter* inclusions.

Modeled after the 1718 hymn book, the 1744 *Psalterspiel* included rubrics almost identical with its 1718 predecessor. There was a church year section, followed by hymns which traced the "Order of Salvation." Of particular interest are the subjects in the second category which have a decidedly Pietist and Brethren stamp. The following is a listing of the "Order of Salvation" rubrics with the number of hymns for each indicated.

>   Of human misery and damnation: 8
>   Of the true repentance and conversion: 10
>   Of the true faith: 9
>   Of holy Baptism: 4

Of the love of Jesus: 23
Of brotherly and universal love: 6
Of Foot-washing and the Love-feast: 1
Of the holy Supper and the proclamation of the death of Jesus Christ on the cross: 7
Of following Jesus: 7
Of the benevolence of God: 10
Of the inner and outer Word: 7
Of the true and the false Christendom: 7
Of the Christian life and conduct: 47
Of Spiritual watchfulness: 18
Of Spiritual battle and victory: 21
Of denial of the world and self: 26
Of the desire for God and Christ: 32
Of Christian resignation: 8
Of the heart's complete surrender to God: 7
Of divine peace and rest of the soul: 8
Of the joy in the Holy Ghost: 15
Of the praise of God: 20
Of the hope of Zion: 23
Of death and resurrection: 6
Of heaven and the heavenly Jerusalem: 22.[41]

Das Kleine Davidische Psalterspiel der Kinder Zions was not only used by the Brethren, the hymn book became the favored collection for many of the German speaking groups in America. It was reprinted many times well into the nineteenth century.[42]

---

[41] H. Durnbaugh, *German Hymnody of the Brethren*, 46–47. As mentioned earlier, Stoffer, discussing the prominent themes of colonial Brethren devotional material, including hymns and edifying works, lists loving communion with God, the denial of self with the world, perseverance in the Christian life, eternal salvation and judgment, and frequent reference to Christ's life and work. *Brethren Doctrines*, 89.

[42] In addition to the 1744 publication, Christopher Sauer Jr. published three more editions (1760, 1764, and 1777). Other American editions were those

Unlike the 1720 hymnal, the 1744 *Psalterspiel* contained many of the traditional features of hymnals: title page, preface, a topical index, an index to the melodies,[43] and an index of first lines. The hymns themselves were arranged in alphabetical order.

Alexander Mack Jr. (1712–1803)

Of special note is the inclusion in the first edition of the *Psalterspiel* of two appendices, the second of which presented the hymn "*Wo Bleiben Meine Sinnen*" *(My Senses are Failing Me)*, attributed by Abraham H. Cassel (1820–1908), the nineteenth century Pennsylvania German book collector, to Alexander Mack Jr., the most literary man of the Brethren in the eighteenth century. The hymn is a teaching hymn in seven parts (with a total of 110 stanzas) on the passion of Christ. All subsequent editions and reprints of the *Psalterspiel* included it in full.[44] The hymn, given in prose translation by Hedda Durnbaugh, begins: "Where have my senses gone? How dim is my mind! What is my heart to do? Who will tell me about the

---

published by Steiner and Cist (1781), Samuel Sauer (1791, 1795, 1797), Michael Billmeyer (1797, 1813, 1817), Schaefer and Maud (1816), Heinrich Ritter (1829), and George Mentz and Son (1833 and frequently thereafter until 1850). Discussed in Nevin W. Fisher, *The History of Brethren Hymnbooks* (Bridgewater, VA: Beacon, 1950), 7.

[43] Regarding the names of the tunes used in the *Psalterspiel*, Nevin Fisher made a comparison of them with the names of the *371 Harmonized Chorales of J. S. Bach* (NY: Holt, Rinehart and Winston, Inc., 1966). Of the ninety-one melodies indicated in the *Psalterspiel*, fifty-three of them also appear in the Bach collection. They are listed in Fisher's *History of Brethren Hymnbooks*, 5–6. The tune names used most frequently were LOBE DEN HERREN (for hymns 68 and 138), JESU MEINE FREUDE (hymns 242–248), NUN DANKET ALLE GOTT (hymns 74, 176, 208), and WACHET AUF! RUFT UNS DIE STIMME DER WÄCHTER (for hymns 44, 117, 123, 178, 252).

[44] H. T. Durnbaugh, *German Hymnody of the Brethren*, 49–50.

wonderful bridegroom who is nailed to the cross, bleeding, as our Pascal Lamb?"

Whether or not this poem actually was intended to be sung is an intriguing question. Perhaps that was the intent. A look at other poetry by Alexander Mack Jr. in other publications of his works reveals the existence of tune names.[45]

Alexander Mack Jr.'s poetry is contemplative and often didactic. The chief concern is pious living, the source of inspiration being the holy Scriptures, as seen in stanzas one and two of a twenty-stanza hymn issued by Christopher Sauer Jr. in 1760, the scriptural allusions being found in Psalm 139, Daniel 5:23, Acts 17:28, and Ephesians 1:22–23.

> *Thou searchest me,*
> *O Lord, how wondrously!*
> *Thou provest me within,*
> *And all my senses, too.*
> *Whatever I may do,*
> *Lying down or standing up,*
> *It happens in Thy presence,*
> *Of this I am aware.*
>
> *O blessed Lord, my Light,*
> *Whate'er my tongue doth speak*
> *Is not concealed from Thee;*
> *Before I am aware,*
> *Or ever have considered,*
> *The word has fled already*
> *And is within Thy power,*
> *Because of Thy great works.*[46]

---

[45] See Samuel B. Heckman, *The Religious Poetry of Alexander Mack, Jr.* (Elgin, IL: Brethren Publishing House, 1912).

[46] Ibid., 25.

While we do not find much of Mack Jr.'s hymnic activity in Brethren hymnals, most likely because they are so introspective and less suitable for the corporate assembly, being aware of his poetry helps to understand the spiritual inclinations and devotional character of the Brethren during this period in the hymns they selected and used.

A couple of further examples which echo distinctive Brethren themes are found in a collection of short poems intended to be sung, issued by Peter Leibert (1727–1812) in 1795. Leibert had been an apprentice to Christopher Sauer Sr., and married a sister of the wife of Alexander Mack Jr.

> *A soul which loves God*
> *Finds anguish in this world.*
> *What it lives outside of Jesus*
> *Is beset by terror and distress.*
> *Therefore Jesus calls to it*
> *"Come, in me is joy and peace."*[47]

> *When the winds of misfortune roar*
> *And the waves of the sea are boisterous,*
> *Then contentment comforts thee.*
> *God, by His holy will, can give again*
> *The life that death has claimed.*
> *This is indeed divine salvation.*[48]

To conclude this glimpse of Mack Jr.'s extra-hymnal activity, it would be appropriate to mention his inclusions in Christopher Sauer Jr.'s *Ein Geistliches Magazein (A Spiritual Magazine)* issued from 1763 to 1772. Headed by a devotional Preface beginning "Worthy Friends and Fellow Pilgrims," an example includes stanzas thirteen and twenty-nine of one of Mack's

---

[47] Ibid., 37.

[48] Ibid., 41.

contributions. They demonstrate Mack's interest in nature themes to shape his thoughts, in this case a call to repentance.

> *We are hurled out of time*
> *Like swift torrents of water*
> *Into the sea of eternity*
> *Where we must forever stay.*
> *O sinner, pause and ponder,*
> *Fall down before your God*
> *In faith and in repentance*
> *While you are allowed to live.*
>
> *Therefore, take courage*
> *You greatly troubled souls,*
> *Be through the blood of Christ*
> *Sharers of Jacob's blessing.*
> *Overcome your own conditions,*
> *Give God alone the honor.*
> *Give ear unto His Word*
> *And seek the Father's home.*[49]

It is worth noting that in these examples from *Das Kleine Davidische Psalterspiel* and Alexander Mack Jr.'s poetry (more given below), social concerns were not the subject of any of the hymns. For the most part the hymns are subjective, contemplative, introspective, didactic, and scriptural, what one would expect from the Pietist points of view the Brethren held in the eighteenth century. The call to pious living on the one hand (the inner life), and the appeal to repentance and salvation on the other (the outer life in the sense of evangelistic activity)

---

[49] Ibid., 145, 153; the Preface is given on 137 & 139; the *Magazine* is further discussed on 120–121.

characterized the hymnody written and used by the Brethren in their Emerging era.[50]

Worship

As mentioned above, the early Brethren met for worship in homes. The basic pattern of their services resembled those of the Pietists in Europe, which included singing, praying, and reading and interpretation of Scripture. One critical observer in 1761, describing mid-eighteenth century Brethren worship, commented:

> Their meetings are zealous and their preaching and praying often take place with great clamor, as if their God were hard of hearing. One hymn chases another as if they lack [inner] silence. They teach their truths after the letter.[51]

In a more complementary way, we may say the Brethren sang many hymns in their worship services, and their singing was energetic, as described by converts.[52]

---

[50] In his conclusion to this period, Stoffer summarizes the colonial Brethren search for a "balance or middle-way between inner and outer expressions of faith." He offers a listing comparing aspects of the inward thought and outward practice of the colonial Brethren. See Stoffer, *Brethren Doctrines*, 97. In addition, Hedda Durnbaugh offers further analysis of the hymnody. "With respect to their German hymnody, the discrepancy between teaching and practice, theology and piety, is immediately obvious. The greater portion of this hymnody bears neither the stamp of Anabaptism nor of Radical Pietism but of that style of conservative, 'churchly' Pietism which is associated with the circle around Francke and Freylinghausen at Halle." Given in Hedwig T. Durnbaugh, "Changes Reflected in Brethren Hymnody: Trends and Implications," *Brethren in Transition: Twentieth Century Directives and Dilemmas*, ed. Emmert F. Bittlinger (Camden, ME: Pemobscot Press, 1992), 199.

[51] D. Durnbaugh, *The Brethren in Colonial America*, 123–124.

[52] D. Durnbaugh, *Fruit of the Vine*, 104.

Singing in worship, which was also a part of baptismal services and Love Feasts,[53] was in unison, unaccompanied, and rendered slowly to ensure clarity of understanding. That their aversion to the use of musical instruments was strong was documented in a letter in 1750 by the Brethren in response to the Moravian Joseph Müller (1707–1761) who expressed a desire that Anabaptist communities of faith be united. The lengthy reply, signed by about thirty Brethren, including Peter Becker and Alexander Mack Jr., read in part:

> The piety which you and your present congregation practice with fiddles, organs, flutes, oboes, bass fiddles, bagpipes, and such nonsense, and infant baptism and your abominable leaders, all of these are so suspicious to us that we consider the whole affair an abominable soup from which we do not wish to taste a single drop.[54]

Die Kleine Harfe (1792)

1792 marked the date of the first Brethren hymnal supplement, *Die Kleine Harfe (The Small Harp)*, published by Samuel Sauer (1767–1820) at Chestnut Hill, Pennsylvania. The supplement contained fifty-eight hymns and was bound with *Das Kleine Davidische Psalterspiel*. No foreword or rubrics were provided, only an index of first lines. It was unique in that it was divided into eight sections representing the eight strings of a Davidic harp, with two morning and two evening hymns added. The second edition published by Samuel Sauer of Baltimore in 1797 included the names of several Brethren authors.[55]

---

[53] Ibid., 186; and Stoffer, *Brethren Doctrines*, 90.

[54] Durnbaugh, *The Brethren in Colonial America*, 312–313.

[55] Two hymns in *Die Kleine Harfe* are from the pen of Johann Conrad Beissel (1691–1768), who left the Brethren and founded a monastic community at Ephratah, Pennsylvania. Also included are one hymn each by two of the sisters

Peter Becker (1687–1758)

The head of the Germantown congregation prior to the arrival of Alexander Mack Sr., Peter Becker, was described as the most gifted singer in the colonial church.[56] Translated by J. S. Flory, Becker's "Thou, Poor Pilgrim" is more of a poem than verse which may be sung. Nevertheless, its inclusion is significant, for it carries again the theme of the suffering pilgrim in need of patience to hold the course of the narrow way. Given here are the first and last of the fourteen stanzas.

> *Thou, poor pilgrim, wander'st here*
> *In this vale of gloom,*
> *Seeking, longing ever more*
> *For that joyous home;*
> *Yet many friends oppose thee here*
> *So that now thou weepest sore - patience.*
>
> *Ah, precious soul, take courage new,*
> *All this shall have an end;*
> *The cross's load will grace renew;*
> *Soon blissful rest thou'lt find.*
> *The sorrow of this fleeting time*
> *Is worthy of the joy divine - patience.*[57]

Jakob Danner (1727–c.1800)

Jakob Danner served as an elder in Pennsylvania and Maryland.[58] His hymn for the dying, *Gute Nacht, ihr Meine*

---

of the community: Sister Naëmi (Naomi Eicher) and Sister Jaël (Barbara Meyer). H. T. Durnbaugh, *German Hymnody*, 62.

[56] Martin Grove Brumbaugh, *A History of the German Baptist Brethren in Europe and America* (Mount Morris, IL: Brethren Publishing House, 1899), 208.

[57] Flory, *Literary Activity*, 206–208.

[58] Donald F. Durnbaugh, "Jacob, Danner," *The Brethren Encyclopedia*, 362.

Lieben (Friends, Good Night) was included in *Die Kleine Harfe*. Stanza one of the ten reads:

> *Friends, good night to you, my truest;*
> *Cherished friends, good night to you;*
> *Mourners, too, good night, my dearest,*
> *You who weep for one so true;*
> *Though I soon shall leave this vale,*
> *And you lay me in this dale,*
> *I shall see a glorious dawning*
> *As we hail that blessed morning.*

Alexander Mack Jr. (1712–1803)

Three hymns by Alexander Mack Jr. were included. One was written on the death in 1784 of Christopher Sauer Jr., his dear friend and fellow elder. Samuel B. Heckman offered a prose translation of this five stanza hymn, *Nun Bricht der Hütten Haus Entzwei (Now Breaks this House of Earth in Twain)*. The approach of the hymn was to have the deceased speak about his earthly pilgrimage. Heckman's stanza one reads:

> *Now breaks this house of earth in twain,*
> *Now the body can decay;*
> *The pilgrimage is now over;*
> *Now will my spirit recover;*
> *The soul has now won the fight;*
> *My Jesus has overcome the enemy.*
> *To Him alone be the honor.*[59]

The third of the Mack inclusions in *Die Kleine Harfe*, *Jesus Christus, Gottes Sohn (Jesus Christ, God's Only Son)* was translated by Ora Garber and included as Hymn 493 in *The Brethren Hymnal* 1951. In that translation the second stanza,

---

[59] Heckman, *The Religious Poetry of Alexander Mack, Jr.*, 43.

"Bless, O Lord, this Church of Thine," appears first. However, the first stanza appears first in the 1992 *Hymnal: A Worship Book* at Hymn 40, with the original second stanza appearing as the third stanza. Garber's poetic translation of the original first stanza is given here.

> *Jesus Christ, God's only Son,*
> *Praise and honor be to Thee!*
> *Thou the great enthroned One,*
> *'Round whom throngs of angels be.*
> *Many thousand watchers there*
> *Lift up joyful praise and prayer.*

It is readily noticed that this hymn text is a departure from Mack's typical character and suffering pilgrim theme, which explains, in the opinion of this writer, one of the reasons why it was included in *The Brethren Hymnal* (1951) with its more *churchly* approach.

Christopher Sauer Jr. (1721–1784)

Alexander Mack Jr. and his dear friend and co-laborer, Christopher Sauer Jr., had a tradition of writing poems on their birthdays. One such poem written by Sauer on his sixtieth birthday was included in *Die Kleine Harfe*. It is a hymn about the cross, the focus being on the Christian's need for perseverance amidst trials. Written several years after the confiscation of his printing business and property during the American Revolution, *Christen Müssen Sich Hier Schicken (Christians Here Must Suit Themselves)* contains thirteen stanzas, each beginning in order with one of the letters of his name. Translated by Obed Snowberger, the first, ninth and eleventh stanzas are given here.

> *Christians here must suit themselves,*
> *In the cross's narrow path;*
> *Here by patience and by stooping,*
> *We must rise to heaven-wards.*
> *He who hopes with Christ to dwell,*
> *Must the cross remember well:*
> *Those who there will be rewarded,*
> *Crowns of thorns here too will carry.*
>
> *Here there is yet time for working,*
> *Sternly still, the right pursue;*
> *Very soon there will be given,*
> *Great rewards to all the true,*
> *Who with courage ventured on,*
> *And could say, vain world be gone:*
> *With thy tempting pleasures all,*
> *Seeking us to bring to fall.*
>
> *Under many storms of trouble*
> *And temptations great and small*
> *God still knew how to protect me,*
> *That I did not come to fall.*
> *Love to me did still extend,*
> *Wonderful and without end.*
> *Without Him I must have perished,*
> *In the time of great distresses.*[60]

Johannes Naas (1669–1741)

Also included in *Die Kleine Harfe* were two hymns by Johannes Naas, who had been an elder in the Marienborn area of Germany, and later in the Krefeld congregation. He came to

---

[60] Translation included in Donald F. Durnbaugh, *The Brethren in Colonial America*, 569–572; also in Brumbaugh's *History of the Brethren*, 434–437.

41

America with some of his family in 1733, and planted churches in both New Jersey and Pennsylvania.[61]

Eins Betrübt Mich Sehr auf Erden (I Have Felt Great Agitation) is a hymn of eighteen stanzas which includes commentary on the condition of humanity, and offers advice that all turn to Christ. Translated by Ora Garber, stanzas one, two and twelve are as follows:

> *I have felt great agitation*
> *That so few accept salvation.*
> *What then should I undertake?*
> *With large numbers sure to perish,*
> *Forfeiting what they should cherish,*
> *Dare I this concern forsake?*
>
> *How can this still be occurring:*
> *That these people are preferring,*
> *In all ranks of life, to fall,*
> *Scanty thought to heaven giving,*
> *With few choosing Christian living?*
> *How can it occur at all?*
>
> *Sons of men, yourselves reversing,*
> *Mark how Christ your souls is nursing;*
> *Mark with care His ways and deeds.*
> *Truth, Way, Life; how much you need Him!*
> *Truth, Way, Life; oh, hear and heed Him!*
> *This advice meets all your needs.*[62]

---

[61] Donald F. Durnbaugh, "Naas, Johannes," *The Brethren Encyclopedia*, Vol. 2, 909. Naas reported that when he and his family arrived in Philadelphia in 1733, "the brethren and sisters came to meet us in small boats with delicious bread, apples, peaches, and other refreshments of the body, for which we praised the great God publicly on the ship with much singing and resounding prayers." Given in D. Durnbaugh, *Fruit of the Vine*, 69.

The second hymn by Naas, *Heiland meiner Seel (Savior of My Soul)* has seventeen stanzas and is a very personal out-pouring to Jesus, truly in the Pietist stream of hymnody. In Brumbaugh's history is given a prose translation. Stanza one reads:

> *Savior of my soul grant that I choose*
> *Thee and Thy cross in this life,*
> *And that I may surrender myself wholly to Thee.*
> *Grant that I choose this, Savior of my soul.*[63]

It is interesting to compare this with two other poetic renderings. Ora Garber's says:

> *Savior of my soul,*
> *Lead me to enroll*
> *'Neath Thy cross this life I'm living*
> *My full being to Thee giving,*
> *May I thus enroll,*
> *Savior of my soul.*[64]

Lillian Grisso's (1889–1974) free paraphrase of stanzas one, three, eight has made the Naas hymn more accessible for singing.

> *Savior of my soul,*
> *Let me choose Thy goal;*
> *Self to Thee I would surrender,*
> *Choose Thy cross, be Thy contender.*
> *Let me choose Thy goal,*
> *Savior of my soul.*[65]

---

[62] Included in *Brethren Life and Thought* (Vol. XVI, Winter 1971, Number 1): 59–61. A prose translation was given in Brumbaugh's *History*, 126–128.

[63] Brumbaugh, *History*, 129–130.

[64] Given in *Brethren Life and Thought* Vol. XV (Autumn 1970, Number 4): 214–216.

William Beery (1852–1956), of whom we shall speak later, wedded the Grisso text with his tune, JOHN NAAS. *Heiland meiner Seel* was not included in other Brethren hymnals until *Neue Sammlung* (1870), of which we shall discuss later as well.

In addition to the Samuel Sauer second edition of *Die Kleine Harfe* in 1797, third and fourth editions were issued by Michael Billmeyer of Philadelphia in 1813 and 1817. The first edition was printed again by Schäffer and Maud in 1816. A fifth edition was published in 1829 (no publisher given); and a sixth edition was printed by Mentz and Rovoudt in 1830.

Jakob Stoll (1731–1822) and the End of an Era

We mentioned initially that in this Emerging era of Brethren life and hymnody, "the death of Alexander Mack Jr. in 1803 marks the passage of the first group of great men who lent lustre to the early history of the church, and who produced the first important body of our church literature;"[66] and that the "chief metaphor for the spiritual life among the Brethren from Alexander Mack [Sr.] to Jakob Stoll (d. 1822) was the life of a suffering pilgrim in a sinful world."[67] Jakob Stoll, who was an elder in the Conestoga, Pennsylvania congregation, has been described as the "foremost Brethren poet of his own and preceding times."[68] Although not appearing in any hymnals during his life-time, Stoll's hymns first appeared in a collection of his poetry and other devotional writings. *Geistliches Gewürz-Gärtlein Heilsuchender Seelen* (*Spiritual Herb-Garden of the*

---

[65] *The Brethren Hymnal* (1951), hymn 361; also as hymn 549 in *Hymnal: A Worship Book* (1992).

[66] Flory, *Literary Activity*, ix.

[67] Martin, "Spiritual Life," *The Brethren Encyclopedia*, 1209.

[68] This comment is given in the note which accompanies the translation of four of Stoll's hymns by Ora Garber in *Brethren Life and Thought*, Vol XVI (Fall 1971, Number 3): 227.

Soul Seeking Salvation) was published in 1806 at Ephrata, Pennsylvania. Several of the hymns were translated by Ora Garber.[69] The following is an example of the similarity of thought with the other hymn-writers of the Emerging era. From Hymn 1 in the collection, stanzas four and five read:

> *Oh, the world brings naught but sorrow*
> *Which hell holds on grand display*
> *In its dark room 'till tomorrow,*
> *Till the coming judgment day.*
>
> *O dear soul, take counsel thereto*
> *And reverse your course and pace,*
> *For your Christ has come first to you*
> *Offering you His love and grace.*[70]

From Hymn 10 stanzas four and seven speak:

> *Total is my degradation;*
> *Nothing good in me is found;*
> *I deserve complete damnation.*
> *Unless Thy rich grace abound,*
> *Animating me anew,*
> *I am worthless through and through.*
>
> *Dearest Jesus, life the dearest,*
> *Thou dost fully know my strife.*
> *My encircling foes Thou hearest*
> *As they taunt my pilgrim-life.*
> *They would take my hope away.*
> *Steel my faith to meet that day.*[71]

---

[69] The Garber translations were included in *Brethren Life and Thought* Vol. XVI (Fall 1971, Number 3); in *Brethren Life and Thought* Vol. XVII (Spring 1973, Number 2); and in Roger E. Sappington's *The Brethren in the New Nation: A Source Book on the Development of the Church of the Brethren 1785–1865* (Elgin, IL: The Brethren Press, 1976), 445-453.

[70] Given in Sappington, *New Nation*, 446.

Stanzas one and ten of Hymn 13 say:

> *Jesus is my good, my goal,*
> *Best of all eternal graces.*
> *Through Him my uplifted soul*
> *Makes its home in heavenly places.*
> *He's the true light of my heart;*
> *From Him I shall not depart.*
>
> *By my Jesus I shall stay,*
> *Ever to Him safely clinging.*
> *I can walk my pilgrim way,*
> *With the light that He is bringing,*
> *Through grave perils lurking there*
> *Of which one is scarce aware.*[72]

And finally, of particular note is Hymn 20, *O! wie ist die Zeit so Wichtig (Oh How is the Time So Urgent)*. Stanzas two and five are the following:

> *Oh, how is the time so urgent,*
> *Which God cannot give again;*
> *And the world how vain, emergent,*
> *Which is loved too much by man,*
> *That we walk in dull neglecting,*
> *Drearily, with scant reflecting*
> *On how long the time may be*
> *Of God's vast eternity.*
>
> *How important and momentous*
> *Are the days of life's brief span;*
> *Teach me, Jesus, how portentous*
> *Are these days to mortal man.*

---

[71] Ibid., 448.

[72] Ibid., 449–450.

> *All my earthly days respecting,*
> *None but Thee as mine electing*
> *Here upon my pilgrim way,*
> *May I bear the cross someday.*[73]

Stanza two was included as Hymn 428 in *The Brethren Hymnal* (1951), though modified for wedding with the J. S. Bach tune, ALLE MENSCHEN MÜSSEN STERBEN.

> *Oh, how is the time so urgent*
> *Which God gives us only once;*
> *And how is the world so empty,*
> *Which by man is loved too much,*
> *That we all, with dull neglecting,*
> *In it walk as if in dreaming,*
> *Thinking little of the span*
> *Of God's vast eternity.*

While the Brethren during the Emerging era exhibited a vital and creative spirit in their poetry, literature and practice, including hymn writing, few Brethren hymn-writers were gifted in terms of excellence in literary facility. Yet they valued their heritage of hymnic writing and singing, and the way hymns and hymn singing serve to glorify God, edify believers, and sound forth and instill the doctrinal truths of the faith. By the end of the eighteenth century, however, changes were on the horizon, and Brethren worship was trending toward more sobriety, with less of the pietistic zeal and fervor of their beginnings.[74] In 1770 the Germantown congregation erected a meetinghouse. For the most part, however, Brethren continued to meet in homes for worship. It was not until well into the 1800s that meetinghouses were more common.

---

[73] Ibid., 453.

[74] Stoffer, *Brethren Doctrines*, 97.

If the inward communion with God has been truly realized, it will issue in outward communion ... with all kinds of virtues of love.... To love one's neighbor as one's self shows clearly what communion is.

Michael Frantz (1687–1748)

[The hymns and other devotional works] indicate that a quiet, devotional, somewhat mystical spirit continued among the Brethren at least into the third decade of the nineteenth century.... Yet the very fact that the above works used borrowed themes and imagery suggest that this pietistic spirit [was] losing its vitality and certainly its originality ... these works are the last clear representatives of the devotional spirit that was so strong during the previous century.

Dale R. Stoffer

Expanding: Late 18th Century to Mid-19th Century

Referring to the late eighteenth century through the first half of the nineteenth century as an Expanding era in Brethren spirituality and hymnic expression is appropriate for several reasons.

Generally speaking, because Brethren were expanding geographically, and with an increasing population of English speaking Brethren, there was a need for a consolidation of congregations to establish a distinct church identity. In 1836 at the Annual Meeting it was decided to give the Brethren an official name, "The Fraternity of German Baptists." We may ask: What were the inward aspects and outward expressions of Brethren spirituality during this period? Did Brethren hymnody reflect the expanding concerns of the Fraternity? Was there a consolidation of hymnic expressions?

In the first part of the nineteenth century, expressions of the inward beliefs and convictions of the Brethren continued through the writing of hymns and devotional works and the publication of new editions of Brethren hymnbooks. All these served the Brethren in their attempt to stem the tide of changes which were inevitable with the increasing English speaking Brethren population and as a counterbalance to the musical influences such as the camp-meeting song literature which became very popular.

Dale Stoffer commented:

> These works indicate that a quiet, devotional, somewhat mystical spirit continued among the Brethren at least into the third decade of the nineteenth century.... Yet the very fact that the above works used borrowed themes and imagery suggest that this pietistic spirit [was] losing its vitality and certainly its originality ...

these works are the last clear representatives of the devotional spirit that was so strong during the previous century.[75]

The Christian's Duty (1791)

1791 was the year the fifth edition of the first American Brethren hymn book, *Das Kleine Davidische Psalterspiel*, was produced. Numerous editions and reprints were produced up to 1853. The supplement, *Die Kleine Harfe*, was bound with most editions and reprints of the 1797 *Psalterspiel*.

Also in 1791 appeared the first English language hymnal for the Brethren, *The Christian's Duty*, published in Germantown by the Brethren elder and former apprentice in the Sauer printing office, Peter Leibert, who purchased the Sauer printing equipment. The full title of the hymnbook was *The Christian's Duty, exhibited in a series of Hymns: collected from various authors, designed for the worship of God, and for the edification of Christians. Recommended to the serious of all denominations. By the Fraternity of the Baptists.*

With this English language hymnbook began what Hedda Durnbaugh described as the second of two entirely separate tracks of Brethren hymnody in the nineteenth century: the German language hymnody and the English language hymn books.[76] Whereas the predominant type of hymns Brethren sang in the eighteenth century was that of conservative German Pietism, sung to German chorale melodies in unison and without printed notation or accompaniment, beginning with *The Christian's Duty* an entirely new repertoire of hymnody was introduced. The Brethren did not carry over their German hymns into their English language hymnody. The result was the gradual but certain shift to English language hymnody, the

---

[75] Stoffer, *Brethren Doctrines*, 106.

[76] Hedwig T. Durnbaugh, "Changes Reflected in Brethren Hymnody," 193–203.

demise of the Brethren's original hymnic heritage, and with that the concentration of the type of piety the hymns reflected.[77]

Durnbaugh explains that no model has been found as yet for the internal organization of the hymn book.[78] J. S. Flory said the hymns "were collected from various sources and authors."[79] Louis F. Benson (1855–1930), renowned hymnologist and author of *The English Hymn*, stated that a 1784 Baptist hymnbook, *A Collection of Hymns, from various authors, adapted to publick worship: designed for the edification of the pious of all denominations; but more particularly for the use of the Baptist Church in Philadelphia*, "was used in the church of the German Baptist Brethren (Dunkers) already formed at Germantown. It certainly furnished much of the materials of the Brethren's first English hymnbook."[80]

The Preface of *The Christian's Duty* describes why the hymnbook was produced, and indicates that it was drawn from several English language hymnbooks:

> The Reason for printing this Hymn Book is: because of the Inconvenience arising from having several Sorts of Hymn Books in Meeting at once, it was therefore thought prudent to remove this Inconvenience, by collecting the most approved Hymns, of several Books, and reducing them into One small Octavo, with a complete Index, which is wanting in the Hymn Book which we have latterly used; although it was otherwise truly excellent.

---

[77] Ibid., 194.

[78] Hedwig T. Durnbaugh, "1791: A Watershed Year in Brethren Hymnody," *Brethren Life and Thought* Vol. 45 (Summer 2000, No. 3), 100.

[79] J. S. Flory, *Literary Activity*, 282.

[80] Louis F. Benson, *The English Hymn: Its Development and Use in Worship* (Richmond, VA: John Knox Press, 1962), 199–200.

In all, four editions were published, the first three in 1791, 1801, and 1813. In 1816 *The Christian's Duty* was enlarged when John Leibert published *A Selection of* [31] *Hymns, from various authors, supplementary for the use of Christians*. The last printing of *The Christian's Duty* was in 1825, and it was of the original 1791 edition.

The Christian's Duty contained 352 hymns. Of the forty topical headings, there are distinct Brethren themes: eight hymn texts "On Baptism," and nine "For washing feet and the Lord's Supper." Of particular interest is the inclusion of thirty hymn texts under the heading of "Supplication Hymns." Approximately ninety hymns in *The Christian's Duty* are of unknown authorship. It is possible some may have been authored by Brethren.

The hymns were drawn almost entirely from the new English hymnody of the eighteenth century. Of the 365 hymns in the 1801 edition, 116 were from the pen of the Isaac Watts (1674–1748) with his psalms metricized and hymns of "human-composure." Thirty hymns were by Charles Wesley (1707–1788), fourteen by Joseph Hart (1712–1768), and fourteen by John Newton (1725–1807). Together these four writers represented forty-seven per cent of all the hymns in *The Christian's Duty*. Examples of hymns in *The Christian's Duty* which appeared in many hymnals of the nineteenth and twentieth centuries include:

Those by Isaac Watts: Alas, and *Did My Savior Bleed; Am I a Soldier of the Cross?; Come Ye That Love the Lord; From all that Dwell Below the Skies; Our God, Our Help in Ages Past* [the original wording]; *When I can Read my Title Clear*.

And these by Charles Wesley: *Christ the Lord is Risen Today; Come, Thou Long-expected Jesus; Hail the Day that Sees Him Rise; Jesus, Lover of My Soul; Lo! He Comes with Clouds Descending; O for a Thousand Tongues to Sing*.

Other hymns to note which serve to indicate the departure from the German hymnic diet of the eighteenth century include: *Awake my Soul, and With the Sun* by Thomas Ken (1637–1711); *Come, Thou Fount of Every Blessing* by Robert Robinson (1735–1790); *God Moves in a Mysterious Way* by William Cowper (1731–1800); *Guide Me, O Thou Great Jehovah* by William Williams (1717–1791); *How Sweet the Name of Jesus Sounds* and *Precious Bible What a Treasure* by John Newton (1725–1807); *Rock of Ages, Shelter Me* [original wording] by Augustus Toplady (1740–1778); W*hile Shepherds Watched Their Flocks by Night* by Nahum Tate (1652–1715). What melodies were used to sing the hymns in *The Christian's Duty* can only be speculated. Hedda Durnbaugh explained:

> It must be assumed that the melodies were widely known and could be sung without any other aid than the printed reference to the meter ... and the intoning of a suitable tune by the presiding elder, minister, or a congregational song leader. The melodies themselves would have been either English tunes newly composed or adapted for these new texts and introduced in the Colonies along with them, or suitable American folk tunes. Just as was the case with the German hymns, certain melodies were closely linked with certain texts. However, as long as the meter [and the accent] fit, tunes could be used interchangeably, and it is therefore impossible to state with any degree of certainty which melody was sung by the Brethren to which tune.[81]

Theologically we might suggest that in *The Christian's Duty* there was a blend of Calvinistic (Watts) and Arminian (Wesley) positions. This is a different mode of theological thinking than that which is present in the German Pietist hymns of the 1744 *Davidische Psalterspiel*. Two streams, two tracks, two languages,

---

[81] H. T. Durnbaugh, "Music in Worship, 1708–1850," 274.

two theological patterns coexisting among the Brethren by 1791 and through the nineteenth century.

While the hymnody of *The Christian's Duty* is a departure from the eighteenth century German hymns of the Brethren, with their suffering pilgrim motif, it should be said that the themes of many of the hymns are not entirely unlike the German devotional themes of individuals being admonished to bend the knee of their hearts and to be cautious regarding the influences of the world. The following titles demonstrate this.

> *Blessed are the Humble Souls That See,*
> *Blest is the Man Who Shuns the Place,*
> *Broad is the Road that Leads to Death,*
> *Death May Dissolve My Body Now,*
> *I'm not Ashamed to Own My Lord,*
> *Lord, We confess Our Num'rous Faults,*
> *Out of the Depths of Long Distress,*
> *O for an Overcoming Faith,*
> *Plung'd in a Gulf of Dark Despair, and*
> *Ye Sons of Men, a Feeble Race.*

Admittedly, however, the more positive, joyful anticipation of the future with Christ in Heaven is more pronounced, as are what some refer to as the more "churchly" hymns. It would be impossible to overstate the significance that with the publication of *The Christian's Duty* the shift to the English language among the Brethren had commenced. Although the literary approach is markedly different from the German hymns, the balance of inwardness and outwardness of spirituality could not be more wonderfully admonished and expressed than in Watts's hymn, given as Hymn CCLXI in *The Christian's Duty*. Stanzas one and three of the four read:

So let our Lips and Lives express,
The holy Gospel we profess;
So let our works and Virtues shine,
To prove the Doctrine all Divine.

Our Flesh and Sense must be deny'd,
Passion and Envy, Lust and Pride,
Whilst Justice, Temp'rance, Truth and Love,
Our inward Piety approve.

Die Kleine Lieder Sammlung (1826)

Through the nineteenth century there remained, although gradually and increasingly less, the need for hymnbooks in the German language. In 1826 *Die Kleine Lieder Sammlung (The Small Collection of Songs)* was published at Hagerstown, Maryland to meet the need of those who preferred to sing in the German language in worship.

At that time many Brethren considered the editions of *Das Kleine Davidische Psalterspiel* to be large and bulky and inconvenient for traveling. *Die Kleine Lieder Sammlung* was a smaller and condensed German language hymnbook. The first edition of this first pocket-sized hymnbook of the Brethren contained 140 hymns, with 102 of them taken from the *Psalterspiel* and seven from its supplement, *Die Kleine Harfe*. The remainder of the hymns were drawn from other hymnbooks and from unpublished sources.[82] Fourteen hymns were by Gerhardt Tersteegen, nine by Joachim Neander, and eight by Johann Schleffer. Jakob Danner's *Gute Nacht, ihr meine Lieben* mentioned above was included. In all, nineteen editions were produced by eight different publishers between 1826 and 1853, eight of them published by Henry Kurtz (1796–1864).[83]

---

[82] Sappington, *The Brethren in the New Nation*, 410.

[83] H. T. Durnbaugh, *German Hymnody*, 73–74. Henry Kurtz was a German born

A baptismal hymn of possible Brethren authorship was *Die sen Täufling wir (We Bring this Person who Wishes to be Baptized)*. Stanza two speaks of the Father, stanza three gives reference to the Son, and stanza four prays to the Holy Spirit, clear referencing to trine immersion. A portion of the hymn as translated by Hedda Durnbaugh, reads:

> Immersed are you in accordance with the word of God in the name of the Son, that you might forever love him from your heart. Amen! Amen! Holy Spirit, may you be well pleased with this our hope![84]

Included in this collection are twelve hymns known to have been used as German bush-meeting songs. Thus, the nineteenth century American camp-meeting spirituals were having an influence on Brethren hymnody, in this case the German hymnody. One example is *Was hat uns doch bewogen (What is It That Has Led Us)* by a newly introduced Brethren hymnwriter, Heinrich Danner (1742–1814), brother to Jakob Danner. The hymn, included in the 1827 edition, consisted of eight stanzas with themes similar to eighteenth century Brethren piety. Translated by Ora Garber, the first and seventh stanzas are given here:

> *What is it that has led us*
> *Away from Germany?*

Lutheran educator, pastor, and publisher who was attracted to the Brethren and eventually became a Brethren elder. He published editions of *Die Kleine Lieder Sammlung* in 1833, 1835, 1837, and 1841 at Osanaburgh, Ohio. At Poland, Ohio he printed editions in 1844, 1848, 1850, and 1853. Extended review of the life and work of Henry Kurtz is given in D. Durnbaugh, *Fruit of the Vine*, 220–222, and in Stoffer, *Brethren Doctrines*, 105–107.

[84] Hedwig T. Durnbaugh, "The Lost Hymns of the Brethren," Report of the Proceedings of the Brethren World Assembly: Elizabethtown College, Elizabethtown, Pennsylvania July 15–July 18, 1992 (Ambler, PA: The Brethren Encyclopedia, Inc., 1994), 6–7.

> *The love of God has sped us*
> *To that community*
> *Which God, the Lord, has founded*
> *In this, a strange new land.*
> *With faith in Him unbounded,*
> *Our lives are in His hand.*
>
> *God wishes to uphold us*
> *In joy and in despair,*
> *That He may yet enfold us*
> *Both here and over there.*
> *He guides the openhearted*
> *Through angels sent to man,*
> *Lest we from Him be parted,*
> *And brings us home again.*[85]

Two new rubrics were introduced in the third edition of 1829: "Hymns of Invitation" (two by Gerhardt Tersteegen),[86] and "Hymns of Awakening" (with Wilhelm Knepper's *Ihr Jungen Helden Aufgewacht* included in this category). Another example of a Hymn of Awakening was an undocumented hymn, *Geh, Seele, Frisch in Glauben fort (Go Forth, My Soul, Renewed in Faith)* of which Hedda Durnbaugh's prose translation of stanzas three and four reads:

> O Jesus, savior of my soul, I come to you without fear; wash off my sin, Emmanuel, O do come to me yourself! Forgive my transgressions, and that which eats away at my heart, and grant me, O Jesus, your grace that I might be undaunted.[87]

---

[85] D. Durnbaugh, *The Brethren in Colonial America*, 558–560.
[86] H. T. Durnbaugh, *German Hymnody*, 69.
[87] Ibid.

A Choice Selection of Hymns (1830)

Die Kleine Lieder Sammlung was followed in 1830 by a new English language hymnbook, *A Choice Selection of Hymns*. These hymnbooks, as Donald R. Hinks remarks, "were destined to replace the *Psalterspiel* and *The Christian's Duty*."[88]

A Choice Selection of Hymns was first published in Canton, Ohio by John Saxton. Henry Kurtz published a second edition in 1833 and several later editions. To service both the German speaking and English speaking Brethren, often *Die Kleine Lieder Sammlung* and *A Choice Selection of Hymns* were bound together, with the German collection preceding the English. Later editions appeared with the order reversed since the English language had become more prominent.[89] That was the case when Henry Kurtz published an 1853 edition of *A Choice Selection of Hymns* bound with an 1853 edition of *Die Kleine Lieder Sammlung*.[90]

Of the 223 hymns in the 1833 edition of *A Choice Selection of Hymns, From Various Authors, Recommended to All Denominations for the Worship of God*, 162 also appeared in the 1825 edition of *The Christian's Duty*, and 43 were found in its 1816 supplement, *A Selection of Hymns*. The remaining hymns were drawn from other sources. This hymnbook served the English speaking Brethren for about thirty years.

Die Kleine Perlen-Sammlung (1858)

German language hymnals continued to be produced through the end of the nineteenth century. However, the contents reflected the changes in the broader congregational singing

---

[88] Donald R. Hinks, *Brethren Hymn Books and Hymnals 1720–1884* (Gettysburg, PA: Brethren Heritage Press, 1986), 47.
[89] Ibid.
[90] Sappington, *New Nation*, 414.

culture in America. In 1858, *Die Kleine Perlen-Sammlung (The Small Collection of Pearls)* was published by J. E. Pfautz at Ephrata, intended to be a supplement to existing hymnals. It included eighty-three hymns, all but one were new to the Brethren hymnic repertoire. Thirty-one were by Brethren authors.

Also present were some traditional hymns and revival songs,[91] the result of the influence of the camp-meeting movement in America since earlier in the century. The official Brethren stance was negative regarding "Protracted [Revival] Meetings." However, the winds of change ultimately were very difficult to hold back. Interestingly, Wilhelm Knepper's *Ihr Jungen Helden, Aufgewacht (Awake, Ye Young Heroes)* from the 1720 hymnal was one of the most popular German camp-meeting songs of the early nineteenth century.[92]

New features in this hymnbook were translations of English hymns. Examples include *Guide Me, O Thou Great Jehovah* by William Williams (1717–1791), and *Hark, Ten Thousand Harps and Voices* by Thomas Kelly (1769–1854) translated by Brethren hymn writer Wilhelm Preiss (1789–1849), the most prolific Brethren hymn writer of the era.

Eleven original hymn texts and five translations of English hymns by Preiss were included.[93] Of his eleven original hymns, *Mein Jesu kaufte mich mit Blut (My Jesus Purchased Me with Blood)* was a typical camp-meeting song with a chorus. We'll cite all four stanzas as paraphrased by Hedda Durnbaugh.

---

[91] Hedwig R. Durnbaugh and Nevin W. Fisher, "Hymnody," *The Brethren Encyclopedia*, Vol. 1, 641.

[92] Hedwig R. Durnbaugh and Nevin W. Fisher, "Hymns," *The Brethren Encyclopedia*, Vol. 1, 643.

[93] H. Durnbaugh, *German Hymnody*, 87.

> *My Jesus purchased me with blood,*
> *He dearly paid for me.*
> *All the wrath of hell engulfed Him.*
>
> *Thus He overcame hell and death for me*
> *And for my benefit.*
> *May He reign in my soul and give me much courage.*
>
> *My Savior, I recognize you,*
> *Because you are white and red.*
> *Yes, your love urges me, which is as strong as death.*
>
> *Yes, your love urges me to long for you*
> *That I, O dear Savior,*
> *May love you there [in eternity] for ever.*[94]

Following each stanza, a chorus was sung, a translation of an English camp-meeting chorus:

> *O the Lamb, the loving Lamb, the Lamb of Calvary,*
> *The Lamb that was slain yet lives again, to intercede for me.*

Another example of a popular chorus, which was attached to many "mother-hymns" of the revival genre, is one following a hymn in this collection by a non-Brethren author, Johannes Walter (1781–1818). The chorus was translated from the English.

> *O that will be joyful, O that will be joyful!*
> *O that will be joyful, To meet to part no more.*[95]

---

[94] Ibid., 88.

[95] Cited in H. Durnbaugh, *German Hymnody*, 83; and given in musical score in Ellen Jane Lorenz, *Glory, Hallelujah! The Story of the Campmeeting Spiritual* (Nashville, TN: Abingdon, 1978), 88.

Other hymn texts by Brethren writers or those attributed to Brethren represented in *Die Kleine Perlen-Sammlung* include those by: Christian Bamberger (1801–1880); Heinrich Danner (1742–before 1814); David Gerlach (c.1811–1879); Samuel Grebil (1809–1881); Jakob Haller (c.1777–1865); J. Hoffer, Jakob W. Meyer Sr. (1832–1906); Abraham Miller (d. 1843); S. D. Miller and Jakob Stoll (1731–1822).[96]

The topic which was represented by the greatest number of hymns was "Hymns about death and burial," of which there were thirteen. An emphasis in many hymns was on conversion, such as Jakob Haller's teaching hymn about the love of Jesus. The seventeen stanzas focus on Brethren distinctives; for example:

From Stanza Five:

> *Jesus' love also commands to keep the covenant of baptism.*

From Stanza Six:

> *Jesus' love is so sweet that it washes*
> *the disciples' feet so that one*
> *Would follow Him even though it is*
> *quite humiliating to do so.*

And from Stanza Seven:

> *Jesus' love takes bread and wine.*
> *Whoever wishes to be His disciple*
> *Must follow His examples in all things*
> *And obey all His teachings.*[97]

---

[96] H. Durnbaugh, *German Hymnody*, 84–89.
[97] Ibid., 85.

Nineteenth Century Brethren Spirituality, Worship and Music Practices

The difference in Brethren spirituality between the eighteenth and nineteenth centuries is described by Dennis D. Martin:

> The spirituality of the suffering pilgrim through a temptation-filled world became formalized in the various symbols of Brethren sectarianism and non-conformity. Brethren nurtured in their children a love for this Brethren way, encouraging a spirituality that was articulated in deeds, not pious or spiritual phrases.[98]

In the first half of the nineteenth century Brethren strove to maintain as much of their original piety as possible. Due to the need for consolidation of congregations, and the felt need to hold on to the Brethren way, rulings regarding behavior were made at the Annual Meetings. In particular, the notion of "separation from the world" led to many official rulings. Carl F. Bowman listed thirty-four of the Brethren 'taboos' spanning 1778 to 1850. Some of them were: dressing fashionably (1804); shaving off beards [for elders] (1804); college education (1831); singing schools in meetinghouses (1838); Sunday schools (1838); the tinkling of bells (1840); protracted meetings [Revivals] (1842); joining worldly associations (1848); benedictions with uplifted hands (1849); working as a butcher in a market (1850).[99]

Anything related to politics, government, and the courts was a taboo. All these were derived from the Brethren insistence that the inwardness of piety be manifested in outward acts of obedience.[100] Non-conformity with the world, non-resistance, sectarianism, and non-swearing characterized Brethren

---

[98] Dennis D. Martin, "Spiritual Life," *The Brethren Encyclopedia,* Vol. 2, 1210.
[99] Carl F. Bowman, *Brethren Society: The Cultural Transformation of a "Peculiar People"* (Baltimore, MD: The John Hopkins University Press, 1995), 80–86.
[100] Ibid., 84.

spirituality during this period. These "observances" emphasized, in their view, practicing the primitive faith, and were a means of protecting and instilling Brethren identity.[101]

Typical Brethren worship services during this period were orderly, patterned simply according to what they believed to be the primitive church's inclusions of singing, praying, reading Scripture and preaching, which elements were a part of the Pietist meetings leading up to the beginnings of the Brethren movement. One might expect such an order of service to have included the following: *congregational hymn singing*, led by a minister or a deacon; *prayer*, offered by the preacher of the day, and which may be followed by the congregation praying the Lord's Prayer; *scripture reading*, as chosen by the preacher of the day, read by one of the ministers or a deacon; *preaching* on the scripture of the day, developed by the preacher of the day, and sometimes additionally by one or more of the other ministers present;[102] *exhortation*, a word of testimony by one of the younger ministers or deacon, encouraging the congregation to actualize the truths of the sermon in their everyday lives; *congregational hymn* and *closing prayer* offered (or vice versa); the simple prayer was not supposed to be thought of as a formal benediction.[103]

---

[101] See Stoffer, *Brethren Doctrines*, 106–110, for more thorough discussion of "The Devotional Lives of the Brethren" and "Doctrinal Developments," and 112–113 for summary statements regarding Brethren spirituality during the first half of the 19th century.

[102] One account of a worship service in the 1830s included a comment which revealed the need and the practice of serving both German speaking and English speaking Brethren. "The services were rather tedious, several discourses were delivered in the German language, and as many in English, after which the deacons bore testimony to what the preachers said." D. Durnbaugh, *Fruit of the Vine*, 194.

[103] Descriptions of typical worship service orders, including the "lining" of hymns, are given in the following: *The Brethren Encyclopedia*, Vol. 2, 1375–

If not included after the first *prayer* of the service, following the *closing prayer* the Lord's Prayer was prayed by the congregation, a practice affirmed by Peter Nead in his *Theological Writings*: "Again, our Prayers ought always to be summed up, or concluded by [praying] the Lord's Prayer; for so Jesus commanded his disciples to do: Luke 11:2."[104]

Carl F. Bowman has appropriately characterized Brethren worship order and practices (Dunker liturgy) as that of liturgical restraint. He says that while it is accurate to say that Brethren were liturgically *plain*, it is equally true that they were plainly *liturgical*. Especially when one considers the several ritual observances of baptism, the love feast, anointing the sick, laying on of hands at baptism and for the installation of ministers, the kneeling posture for prayer during worship with the regular congregational praying of the Lord's Prayer, and greeting one another with the holy kiss; and in spite of the simplicity of the Brethren order of the Sunday service, "the Brethren liturgical life can be described as nothing other than rich."[105]

In this Expanding era, the outward expressions of Brethren spirituality included the way Brethren sang and what they were to resist doing, more so than the content of their hymn texts. They maintained their official stance regarding the use of musical instruments. Annual Meeting decisions from 1852 to 1874 went so far as to prohibit ownership or instruction on

---

1376; H. R. Holsinger's *History of the Tunkers and the Brethren Church*, 14, 239–240, 244–249; James H. Lehman, *The Old Brethren*. Second Edition (Elgin, IL: Brethren Press, 2008), 67–74; D. Durnbaugh, *Fruit of the Vine*, 122–123; Carl. F. Bowman, *Brethren Society*, 64–66; and Stoffer, *Brethren Doctrines*, 100, 270 (notes 9 and 10). Excellent descriptions of Brethren Love Feasts (Holy Communion) and the role of hymn singing within them are given in Holsinger's *History*, 249–254; in Sappington, *New Nation*, 188–191; and in Bowman, *Brethren Society*, 58–60.

[104] Peter Nead, *Theological Writings*, 180.

[105] Bowman, *Brethren Society*, 71–73.

musical instruments.[106] The hymns were "lined," often led by a deacon serving as song leader (*Vorsänger*). Hymns were sung slowly and thoughtfully, and every stanza of a hymn was sung.[107] Hymns were supposed to be sung with melody only. However, four-part singing was evidenced among the Brethren,[108] in spite of the fact that in 1844 a report on congregational singing stated that four-part harmony was not acceptable.[109]

Brethren hymnbooks in mid-century continued to be printed without musical notation. According to the Annual Meeting decisions in 1825 and 1838, Brethren were prohibited from providing a meeting place for or teaching in "singing schools" (which taught people to sing by solmization [*do, re, mi,* etc.] or to read music, whether by shape-notes or traditional notation).[110] The prohibition was moderated in later meetings (1862, 1874), most likely due to the fact that some Brethren musicians traveled about as singing school teachers, not the least of whom was the "pioneer Brethren musician," John Cook Ewing (1849–1937), whose "tuning fork" was his sole instrument for teaching in the churches in those days of unaccompanied hymn singing.[111] Brethren hymnals soon would be set with musical notation. We shall speak more of Ewing and tune books in the next two eras.

---

[106] Nevin W. Fisher, "Musical Instruments," *The Brethren Encyclopedia*, Vol. 2, 900.

[107] Holsinger, *History*, 246.

[108] Nevin W. Fisher, "Musical Instruments," *The Brethren Encyclopedia*, Vol. 2, 900.

[109] Nancy Rosenberger Faus, "Singing," *The Brethren Encyclopedia*, Vol. 2, 1185.

[110] Ibid.

[111] Earl C. Kaylor, *Truth Sets Free: Juniata Independent College in Pennsylvania. Founded by the Brethren, 1876. A Centennial History* (New York: A. S. Barnes and Company, 1977), 59.

In the Expanding era, was there a consolidation of hymnody? Certainly attempts were made to service both German speaking and English speaking Brethren by providing hymnbooks for each—sometimes joined in publication—which represented to a certain extent the people being bound together as a distinct fraternity. Did the hymnody reflect the expanding spiritual concerns and rulings of the first half of the century? In this writer's view, not that much. Hymn texts stayed aloof, and focused more on the personal faith characteristics which had been there from the beginning of the "brotherhood". The sense of urgency fostered by the persecutions of the European period had lessened. Were the selection and compilation of both German language and English language Brethren hymnbooks influenced by the larger musical trends of the American musical scene? They most definitely were, and would be influenced to an even greater extent in the next era.

In 1867 the Brethren produced the first officially approved English language hymnbook, described by Hedda Durnbaugh as "the most significant event of the nineteenth century in respect to Brethren hymnody."

John Cook Ewing (1849–1937) was the pioneer Brethren musician, teacher and composer. He served as the first music instructor at Huntingdon Normal School (later Juniata College) and at Ashland College. He was entrusted with the revision of *The Brethren's Tune and Hymn Book* (1879), and compiled *The Brethren Hymnody with Tunes* (1884).

Excepting: Mid-19th Century to the 1880s

Labeling the period of the mid-nineteenth century to the 1880s as Excepting is because of the exceptions "Progressive" and "Traditional" (Conservative) Brethren took with each other over such issues as higher education, missions, a paid ministry, Sunday schools, revivals, prayer meetings, private devotional exercises, social gatherings, collecting an offering during worship, baptizing indoors, the use of musical instruments in worship, and musical notation in hymnbooks. Although instrumental accompaniment for congregational singing was introduced in the Philadelphia congregation in the 1870s, the Annual Meeting took exception to this practice, as well as others, and formally disapproved.[112] Some Brethren families owned pianos or reed organs for the use of accompanying singing in their homes.[113]

Progressive Brethren took exception with the conservatives for not being open to newer practices which they considered beneficial for edification, training, expression, and witness. The more conservative Brethren continued to be cautious about what they considered to be innovations, and took exception with Brethren who, in their view, may have been caving in to the ways of the world. They proposed, for example, that too much education would be corrupting. The positions each group took served to polarize the Brethren, so much so that schism resulted in the 1880s of which Brethren are all aware, resulting in the establishment of three official Brethren groups: the German Baptist Brethren (the cautious Conservatives, renamed the Church of the Brethren in 1908), The Brethren Church (the

---

[112] Nancy Rosenberger Faus, "Singing," *The Brethren Encyclopedia*, Vol. 2, 1185; Carl Bowman gives an account of the objections to the trends in the Philadelphia congregation in the 1860s and 1870s in *Brethren Society*, 106–110.

[113] Faus, "Singing," *The Brethren Encyclopedia*, Vol. 2, 1184.

Progressives), and the Old Order German Baptist Brethren (the Traditionalists, who strongly resisted any changes).[114]

The two dominant and competing forms of piety of this period may be described as "revivalist" and "traditional" (or classical); revivalist piety emphasized personal experience with God and a deep concern for others, and was cultivated in prayer meetings and revival services with gospel singing. The older piety on the other hand resisted any departures from the traditional, classical Brethren thinking and practices.[115] As Carl Bowman interpreted: "Each innovation was linked to more basic understandings of the meaning of faithfulness, the church's identity as a promoter of primitive Christianity, and the whole question of whether the ancient Brethren were really inspired."[116]

A Collection of Psalms, Hymns, and Spiritual Songs (1867) Neue Sammlung (1870)

In 1867 the Brethren produced the first officially approved English language hymnbook, described by Hedda Durnbaugh as the "most significant event of the nineteenth century in respect to Brethren hymnody."[117] After eighteen years of discussion and delay, *A Collection of Psalms, Hymns, and Spiritual Songs; suited to the Various Kinds of Christian worship; and especially designed for, and adapted to, The Fraternity of the Brethren. Compiled by Direction of the Annual Meeting, Upon the Basis of the Hymn Books Formerly used by the Brotherhood* was published at Covington, Ohio by James Quinter (1816–1888),

---

[114] The name of the parent body was officially changed in 1871 from The Fraternity of German Baptists (1836) to the German Baptist Brethren, and later renamed the Church of the Brethren (1908).

[115] Stoffer, *Brethren Doctrines*, 158. See also Dennis D. Martin, "Spiritual Life", *The Brethren Encyclopedia*, Vol. 2, 1210.

[116] Bowman, *Brethren Society*, 108.

[117] H. Durnbaugh, "Changes Reflected in Brethren Hymnody," 197.

Brethren pioneer educator and journalist. He served as the 1867 hymnbook's principal compiler of this words-only, pocket-sized collection of 818 hymns.[118] In addition to his remarks in the Preface, referenced in the introduction to the present study, Quinter commented on the kind of spirituality through hymns he wished to emphasize, that which was valued by the Brethren through the years, especially in the German spiritual milieu.

> Some, looking at a Hymn Book as being designed especially for public worship, and finding that the number of hymns used on occasions of that kind is somewhat limited, think a large number of hymns is objectionable. But when it is remembered that the Bible and Hymn Book constitute the library of some Christians; that the latter is the only book of sacred poetry they possess; that it is not only used as a book to sing from, but is also read and studied with pleasure and profit, the propriety of having some hymns beside those that are popular in the congregation, will be acknowledged. Some Christians who sing but little, and indeed some, who sing not at all, enjoy themselves very much in reading their Hymn Book, and regard it as an excellent companion in retirement.[119]

Of special interest is the inclusion for the first time in Brethren hymnals of an index which contained the names of the authors of the hymn texts when they were known. Perhaps for the purpose of humility, the names of Brethren authors were intentionally not included. The hymn inventory of this hymn book, as with the previous two Brethren English language collections, included many texts by Isaac Watts, Charles Wesley, and Joseph Hart, as well as numerous other writers represented

---

[118] See "Quinter, James" in *The Brethren Encyclopedia,* Vol. 2, 1076–1077, for more on his life and work.

[119] *A Collection of Psalms, Hymns, and Spiritual Songs* (1867), iv. and v.

in *The Christian's Duty*, such as Anne Steele, John Newton, Philip Doddridge, William Cowper and Augustus Toplady. Brethren who took exception to hymnals with musical notation continued to use this collection, reissued from Mt. Morris and Elgin, IL, as late as 1901.[120]

It is worth noting, that while the "pilgrim" theme does not appear as frequently as it did in the Emerging era, it is present in three of the hymns in the 1867 hymn book; Hymn 523, *"Lord, What a Wretched Land is This"* by Isaac Watts; Hymn 524 of unknown authorship, perhaps by a Brethren, *"What Poor, Despised Company,"* included also as 524 in the 1879 hymnbook to be discussed below. The third is Hymn 675, *"My Days are Gliding Swiftly By,"* by Presbyterian clergyman, David Nelson (1793–1844). Stanzas one and four of Nelson's hymn say:

> *My days are gliding swiftly by,*
> *And I a pilgrim stranger,*
> *Would not detain them as they fly—*
> *Those hours of toil and danger.*
>
> *Let sorrow's rudest tempest blow,*
> *Each chord on earth to sever,*
> *Our King says come, and there's our home,*
> *For ever! O, for ever!*

As might be anticipated, exception arose by German speaking Brethren regarding the non-existence of German language hymns in this officially approved hymnbook. In response, the Annual Meeting of 1868 officially directed a committee, which included Henry Kurtz, to produce a collection of modest length, not to exceed 200 hymns. The result was the publication in 1870 of *Neue Sammlung* (*New Collection*), a text-only, pocket-sized

---

[120] See H. R. Durnbaugh and Nevin W. Fisher, "Hymnals," *The Brethren Encyclopedia*, Vol. 1, 642.

hymn book. It exceeded the suggested number of hymns, including 303. *Neue Sammlung von Psalmen, Lobesängen und Geistlichen Liedern (New Collection of Psalms, Songs of Praise and Spiritual Songs)* provided a suitable supplement to *A Collection of Psalms, Hymns, and Spiritual Songs* (1867), and in subsequent printings they were bound together with the English portion occurring first. At the 1872 Annual Meeting both hymnbooks were officially approved for use in Brethren churches.

More English hymns in translation were incorporated in *Neue Sammlung* than in any previous Brethren hymnbook. German Brethren authors included Wilhelm Knepper, Peter Becker, H. Danner, J. Danner, Alexander Mack Jr., Johannes Naas, and Wilhelm Preiss.

Some of the subjects and numbers of hymns in the 1867 hymnbook include the following:

> Death: 53
> Heaven: 34
> Invitation and Warning: 26
> Repentance: 20
> Prayer: 20
> Baptism: 11
> Feet-washing: 6
> Love-Feast: 2
> Anointing: 2.

By way of comparison, within *Neue Sammlung*, we find:

> Christian Belief: 44
> Hymns of Awakening and Invitation: 17
> Penitence, Faith and the New Birth: 13
> Resurrection and Eternal Life: 12
> Death and Burial: 12
> Feet-washing, Love-Feast and Communion: 14
> Baptism: 6

The inclusion of "Hymns of Awakening and Invitation" in *Neue Sammlung* is noticeable, and influenced evidently by the revivalist character within American Christian culture since the beginning of the century. The inordinate amount of hymns on death in the 1867 hymnbook is also pronounced.

Das Christliche Gesang-Buch (1874) Ein Sammlung von Psalmen, Lobesängen, und Geistlichen Liedern (1893)

Still, dissatisfaction continued to be expressed in the Eastern District of Pennsylvania regarding the need for more German language hymns. In 1874 they published their own hymnal of 399 hymns, *Das Christliche Gesang-Buch (The Christian Song Book)*, and reprinted it in 1879. An appendix to the first edition had 82 hymns, 77 of which were by Philipp Friedrich Hiller (1699–1769), the foremost hymn-writer of Württemberg Pietism.

In a few years, the Eastern District of Pennsylvania evidently dissatisfied again with what was not provided for German singing Brethren, produced what would be the last German language hymnbook for the Brethren: *Ein Sammlung von Psalmen, Lobesängen, und Geistlichen Liedern (A Collection of Psalms, Hymns and Spiritual Songs)*, published by The Brethren Publishing Company at Mount Morris, IL in 1893. Two additional editions were printed, one at Mount Morris, IL in 1895 and the other at Elgin, IL in 1903. The categories with the greatest number of hymns included Hymns for Sickness, Death, and Funerals (55), Christ (38), and Invitation (19). The hymns were arranged according to the Order of Salvation. An index of melodies and meters and an alphabetical index of first lines were provided at the end of the volume. With the last printing of *Ein Sammlung*, the German track of Brethren hymnody drew to a close.

Over the course of nearly 200 years of the Brethren, the German hymnals changed in size and increased in the number of hymns and hymn-writers. Physically, the hymnbooks were about half their original size, and the length of hymns was greatly reduced. Whereas in the eighteenth century it was common for hymn texts to have between ten and twenty stanzas, by mid-nineteenth century it was common to write hymns with four to six stanzas.

The known Brethren who composed religious poetry and hymns in the German language number twenty. In alphabetical order, their names, with profession or position, and the number of their known hymns are the following:

>Bamberger, C[hristian] (1801–1880): elder, physician, 2
>Becker, Peter (1687–1758): elder, weaver, 1
>Danner, Heinrich (1742–before 1814): 2
>Danner, Jakob (fl. 1800): elder, 1
>Gerlach, David (c.1811–1879): elder, preacher, 1
>Grebil, Samuel (1809–1881): minister, 1
>Haller, J[akob] (c. 1777–1865): elder, preacher, 1
>Hoffer, J. (19th c., Probably Brethren): 1
>Knepper, Wilhelm (1691–c.1743): weaver, 100
>Kurtz, Heinrich (1796–1874): pastor, publisher, 1
>Mack, Alexander (1679–1735): minister, 1
>Mack, Alexander Jr. (1712–1802): elder, author, 24
>Meyer, Jakob (1832–1906): elder, 3
>Miller, A[braham] (d. 1843): minister, 1
>Miller, S. D. (19th c.): 5
>Naas, Johannes (1669–1743): minister, 2
>Preiss, Johannes (1702–1724): poet, 13
>Preiss, Wilhelm (1789–1849): elder, musician, poet, teacher, 14 original texts and translations
>Sauer, Christoph Jr. (1721–1784): elder, printer, 1
>Stoll, Jakob (1731–1822): elder, author, weaver, 24.[121]

---

[121] H. T. Durnbaugh, *German Hymnody*, 135–136, 285–296.

Further, comparison of the rubrics between the earlier German and English language hymn books, *Das Kleine Davidische Psalterspiel* (1744) and *The Christian's Duty* (1791), with those of *Neue Sammlung* (1870) and *A Collection of Psalms, Hymns and Spiritual Songs* (1867), serves to highlight the similarities and differences in the hymnic spiritual themes of the Brethren during the gradual shift from German language hymnody to English language hymnbooks. Overall, the hymns in the *Psalterspiel* (1744) were more richly doctrinally-oriented (e.g. Order of Salvation), and in the *Collection* (1867) there is more of a balance between the doctrinal hymns and those focusing on practical theological concerns. In the English language hymnbooks prominent themes include Christ's life and mission, Christ's coming again, repentance and conversion, supplication, public worship, hymns of awakening and invitation, family, and death (53 of the 60 on death and resurrection being on death). In the German language hymnals there is more attention given to love of Jesus, the mystery of the cross, spiritual watchfulness, spiritual battle and victory, denial of self and the world, desire for Christ, joyfulness in faith, and true and false Christendom. To say this another way, change over time in the German hymnbooks is seen with increased inclusion of hymns on death and resurrection, and awakening and invitation, while the English hymnals saw an increase in hymns of worship and praise, death and resurrection, awakening and invitation, and family.

The Brethren's Tune and Hymn Book (1872, 1879) John Cook Ewing (1849–1937)

Unlike *A Collection of Psalms, Hymns, and Spiritual Songs* (1867) and *Neue Sammlung* (1870), the first Brethren hymnal with musical notation was published without official direction by the Annual Meeting. *The Brethren's Tune and Hymn Book* of 1872 was an unsuccessful attempt to introduce a hymnal with musical notation, utilizing shape-notes. The hymns were set in three-part harmony, with the melody in the middle (or tenor part). The hymn texts were almost the same as those of the 1867 hymnbook, but that did not ensure its acceptance. Hedda Durnbaugh explained:

> The chief problem with this tune book was that it did not represent what the majority of the Brethren sang during the second half of the 19th century but what some people in the Shenandoah Valley liked to sing. The music ... stood in the tradition of folk and camp-meeting songs. The tunes and especially their three or four-part arrangements in seven-shape notation reflected the singing style of singing-schools and social gatherings.[122]

The unpopularity of the 1872 tune book was most likely enhanced because it was published, along with Benjamin Funk (1829–1909), by "progressive" H. R. Holsinger (1833–1905), with whose views many took exception. Regarding the use of musical notation, the following query was raised at the Annual Meeting in 1873: "Do the Brethren not think it proper to exert their influence against the admission into the church of a new Hymn Book with notes?" An official reply stated: "We advise all districts of the churches to keep [the tune book] out of the church in public worship."[123]

An attempt was made to issue a "carefully revised, re-arranged and otherwise improved"[124] edition in 1879, published by James Quinter and H. B. and J. B. Brumbaugh. It was still set in shape-notation, but this time in four-part harmony. There was a more positive response, although the denomination neither sanctioned nor denounced the book. Much credit for the success of this tune and hymn book must be given to John Cook Ewing

---

[122] H. T. Durnbaugh, "Changes Reflected in Brethren Hymnody," 198.

[123] 1873 *Minutes of the Annual Meeting*, Article 20, p. 312.

[124] From the Title page of *The Brethren's Tune and Hymn Book* (1879).

(1849–1937) who was enlisted to make the revision. He was the first music instructor at Huntingdon Normal School (later Juniata College) and conducted singing classes in many locations.[125]

Because this was such a significant "moment" in the history of Brethren spirituality and hymnody, and because J. C. Ewing was the person who facilitated the success of the revision and who paved the way for future Brethren musicians and hymnal production while a member of the German Baptist Brethren and later The Brethren Church, we include here and in the next chapter a few remarks made about this special musician, who was a fine organist, pianist and vocal teacher, respected college instructor, public school music supervisor and teacher, and faithful parish musician.

The *Primitive Christian and Pilgrim*, a sixteen page weekly newspaper edited by James Quinter, documented Ewing's presence at Juniata, his expertise, and his engagement in the 1879 revision.

> The [Music] department is conducted by Bro. J. C. Ewing of Ohio, who comes to us highly recommended as a teacher of Music, both Vocal and Instrumental. He has been under the instructions of some of the best teachers in the country. [He is] rendering good assistance in preparing our revised Tune Book for the press. He is well informed in the science of music, and

---

[125] A photo of John Cook Ewing with the other members of the first faculty at Juniata, and photos and description of William Beery (1852-1956), Ewing's successor, are given in David Emmert's *Reminiscences of Juniata College, 1876-1901* (Huntingdon, PA: Published by the Author, 1901), 125-126 (Beery), 131 (Ewing in the 1878 Faculty Group), 157 (Beery in the 1901 Faculty). Description of Ewing is given in Earl C. Kaylor's *Truth Sets Free*, 59.

> the Church can look for a book, in every way worthy of patronage.[126]
>
> Bro. J. C. Ewing contemplates spending vacation in Somerset Co., where the brethren promise to raise him several large singing classes. We trust his experience will be more than realized. Bro. Ewing is a fine musician and those who put themselves under his instructions cannot fail to make rapid progress in the science that he knows so well how to teach. He has a special fondness for teaching vocal music and is anxious to do all in his power to make this branch of education more popular among the Brethren. We ought to encourage him in this desire, especially since we, as a body, do not encourage the introduction of instrumental music. We all believe in singing, but very few of us know what it is to "sing with the spirit and *with the* UNDERSTANDING also."[127]

Music education, one of the matters the Progressive Brethren advocated, and with which the church up to this point took exception, was beginning to take hold, as seen in the 1891 edition of the 1879 tune book. At the beginning of the book appeared four pages of the rudiments of music, with an explanation of singing by the shape-note system of musical notation advanced by the singing school tradition.

287 tunes were used for the tune book's 818 hymns. Occurring in some of the tunes was a greater usage of the more lively dotted eighth and sixteenth-note patterns, common to the increasingly popular gospel songs which will appear in more Brethren hymnbooks forthcoming. Hedda Durnbaugh comments: "If what and how the Brethren at large sang at the

---

[126] *Primitive Christian and Pilgrim*, Huntingdon, PA (Tuesday, October 2, 1877, Vol. 1, No. 39): 607, 611.

[127] *Primitive Christian and Pilgrim*, Huntingdon, PA (Tuesday, December 18, 1877, Vol. 1, No. 50): 779.

time was indeed reflected in the second edition of this first Brethren tune and hymn book, then well before the third quarter of the nineteenth century they sang very much the style of hymn one finds in *The Brethren Hymnal* (1951) with the exception of the gospel songs, which date from a later period."[128] Included in the hymnbook were seventeen original tunes by Ewing, and two (CHERWELL at 812 and COOK for 818) by his student and successor at Juniata, William Beery (1852–1956). With Ewing, Beery and other musicians who followed them, the era of Brethren hymn tune composers took flight.[129]

A Collection of Hymns and Sacred Songs (1882)

With the divisions of the Brethren in the early 1880s came two new hymnbooks. The first is mentioned in this chapter because in Brethren hymnody it represents the "old ways" and indicates the cautions and some of the exceptions of this period. The second will be discussed at the beginning of the next chapter.

In 1882 the Old German Baptist Brethren produced *A Collection of Hymns and Sacred Songs suited to Both Private and Public Devotions* adapted to the wants and uses of the Brethren in the Old German Baptist Church, published at the office of *The Vindicator*: Kinsey's Station, Ohio [near Dayton]. Of the 558

---

[128] H. T. Durnbaugh, "Changes Reflected in Brethren Hymnody," 198.

[129] An account of the life and work of J. C. Ewing and a thorough examination of his hymn tunes is given in *John Cook Ewing (1849–1947): Pioneer Brethren Musician, Teacher and Composer* by William Berry (1852–1956) and Peter E. Roussakis (Kokomo, IN: Meetinghouse Press, 2010). This is the first publication of Berry's heretofore unpublished 1942 manuscript of the life and work of J. C. Ewing, and it is supplemented by a musical analysis of Ewing's tunes by Peter E. Roussakis. Within the 1879 hymnal itself, there is no indication of which tunes were composed by Ewing and Beery. However, William Beery later gave an account of them in his booklet, *Brethren Hymns, Hymnals, Authors and Composers: A Study in Our Literary and Musical Heritage* (Elgin, IL: Board of Christian Education, Church of the Brethren, 1945), 6–7.

English language, text-only hymns, 313 were drawn from the Brethren hymnbook of 1867, which means many hymns by Watts and Wesley are present. Also included were nineteen hymn texts by Elder Samuel Kinsey (1832–1883), one of the members of the hymnbook committee.

Kinsey's hymns were drawn from two of his previous publications, *Original Hymns* (1858), and *The Pious Companion* (1865), and from *The Vindicator*, begun by Kinsey in 1870 and which became the official periodical of the Old German Baptist Church. With minor changes and printings through the years, *A Collection of Hymns and Sacred Songs* continues to be used by the Old German Baptist Brethren (also referred to as the Old German Baptist Church).

Elder Kinsey's poetry is straightforward, advancing traditional Brethren themes; for example, obedience, self-denial, and their reward in Hymn 241.

> *Oh, who would not a Christian be,*
> *The Lord of life and glory see;*
> *Obey His word out of true love,*
> *And meet the blessed saints above.*
>
> *To serve our God, oh, let us try,*
> *Uphold his cause, all self deny;*
> *That when our days are number'd here,*
> *We may in heaven with Christ appear.*

Several of Kinsey's texts speak of the Brethren ordinances, two on feet-washing (Hymns 309, 311), one on anointing (Hymn 322), and two on the holy kiss (Hymns 304, 305). All are given in the nature of admonitions, as are the four stanzas of the salutation Hymn 304.

Greet one another with a kiss,
Ye follow'rs of the Lord;
Take up the cross, ye friends of bliss,
Trust ever in his word.

"Greet one another with a kiss
Of love and charity;"
Th' Apostle Paul four times saith this,
To those who'd Christians be.

"Greet one another with a kiss,"
Hear Peter, also, say;
How can we show more love than this,
When we our God obey.

Ye then who would religious be,
And make sure work for heav'n,
With Paul and Peter, too, must see
The plan by Jesus giv'n.

Energizing: The 1880s to Early 20th Century

After the divisions, the long-standing opposition to revivals and many other matters continued to be the position of the Old German Baptist Brethren. The popularity of the gospel song genre, however, became a major ingredient not only in the hymnody of The Brethren Church, newly formed in 1883, but also in the German Baptist Brethren (Church of the Brethren). The revivalist piety,[130] which had been growing since the mid-century, was served well by what seemed to be a prevalent opinion "that hymns should be of a devotional rather than a doctrinal nature."[131] While the controversies and divisions may be viewed negatively, and not without great pain, the 1880s through the early twentieth century was also a period of energizing. Freedom to move onward must have been sensed by both the German Baptist Brethren and The Brethren Church. Many of the negatives of the past were turned into positives by both fellowships, as in the activity of hymnbook production, other song book publications, and hymn tune composition by Brethren musicians.

The Brethren Hymnody with Tunes (1884) John Cook Ewing (1849–1937)

The second hymnbook produced as a result of the divisions was *The Brethren Hymnody with Tunes for the Sanctuary, Sunday School, Prayer Meeting, and Home Circle* published for The Brethren Church in 1884, the first officially sanctioned denominational hymnbook of the Brethren with round note musical notation.[132]

---

[130] A summary of the characteristics of the revivalist piety is given in Stoffer, *Brethren Doctrines*, 158–160.

[131] Hedwig T. Durnbaugh, "The Lost Hymns of the Brethren, 1720–1880," 27.

[132] Unofficially, the first hymnbook by any Brethren using round note musical notation was produced by David F. Eby (1828–1917), Church of the Brethren

The title says it all, that these Brethren desired to move onward in the ways they worshiped, studied, and nurtured their piety. While this writer would most definitely agree with Louis F. Benson's analysis that this modest-sized hymnbook was "a much inferior [hymn] book,"[133] it represented the changes which had taken place regarding Brethren Church thought and practice, and which would burst into full bloom in the Church of the Brethren. *The Brethren Hymnody with Tunes* represents a significant "energizing" of the Brethren to move forward, to evangelize, to make disciples, and above all, to "enjoy" being Brethren Christians, focusing less in hymnody on death and dreariness, and more upon resurrection and the hope we profess because of our faith in, and fellowship with, Jesus.

Directed by the first Brethren Church denominational meeting in Dayton, Ohio in 1883, John Cook Ewing (who referred to himself as J. C. Ewing), who had been entrusted with the 1879 revision of *The Brethren's Tune and Hymn Book*, and who aligned himself with The Brethren Church, was called upon to compile the *Hymnody*, which he published in 1884 at Wilmington, Ohio. He was also called upon to serve as the first music instructor at Ashland College.[134]

Of the 324 entries in *The Brethren Hymnody with Tunes*, thirty were of the gospel song genre. The hymnbook, which has an Index of Subjects and an Index of First Lines, was divided into three sections. Part I is described as a collection of standard metrical hymns and tunes of the more objective variety. For example, the lead hymn of Part I is Edward Perronet's *"All Hail*

---

elder, who compiled *Bible School Echoes and Sacred Hymns*, published by the Brethren at Work Publishing Co., Lanark, IL in 1880. It contained 210 hymns using 97 tunes.

[133] Louis F. Benson, *The English Hymn*, 366.

[134] Clara Worst Miller and Edward Glenn Mason, *History of Ashland College 1878-1953*, Arthur P. Petit, ed. (Ashland, OH: The Ashland College Diamond Jubilee Committee, 1953), 20.

the Power of Jesus' Name." Among other standard familiar hymn texts in Part I are six by Charles Wesley (e.g. Hymn 20, *"A Charge to Keep I Have,"* and Hymn 55, *"Jesus, Lover of My Soul"*); nine by Isaac Watts (e.g. Hymn 60, *"Jesus Shall Reign,"* Hymn 72, *"When I Survey the Wondrous Cross,"* and Hymn 110, *"O God, Our Help in Ages Past"*); John Newton's Hymn 33, *"Glorious Things of Thee are Spoken,"* and Hymn 118, *"Amazing Grace";* Augustus Toplady's *"Rock of Ages"* as Hymn 82; and William Cowper's *"There is a Fountain Filled with Blood"* at Hymn 160.

Ewing contributed four tunes to this section, one being ASHLAND set to a text of unknown authorship, *"Almighty Sov'reign of the Skies."* The significance of this tune lies in the fact that years later for *The Brethren Hymnal* (1951), noted Church of the Brethren music professor at Bridgewater College, Nevin W. Fisher (1900–1984), arranged the tune and wedded it with the lead text of the 1867 *Collection* and *The Brethren's Tune and Hymn Book* (1879), *"Is There a God?"* the text being altered by Kenneth I. Morse (1913–1999). The much improved tune was renamed PIONEER by Fisher in honor of J. C. Ewing.

Part II of *The Brethren Hymnody with Tunes* includes many of the then more popular gospel hymns, most with the stanza and chorus format, songs which were intended by Ewing for wider usage in Sunday schools, prayer meetings, and the home circle. This section includes such well-known gospel hymns as *"What a Friend We have in Jesus"* (Hymn 238), *"Sweet By and By"* (265), and *"Near the Cross"* (308). However, most of the inclusions in this section are very unfamiliar and do not occur in most hymnals of the twentieth century. Ewing contributed fourteen tunes to this section.[135] The hymn texts for which he set music

---

[135] All of J. C. Ewing's tunes in the 1879 revision and in *The Brethren Hymnody with Tunes* are shown and discussed in William Beery and Peter E. Roussakis, *John Cook Ewing (1849–1937)*.

are all of the subjective, personal piety type, as with Hymn 297, Fanny Crosby's children's hymn, *"If I Come to Jesus."* Of the four stanzas, the first says:

> *If I come to Jesus,*
> *He will make me glad;*
> *He will give me pleasure,*
> *When my heart is sad.*
> *If I come to Jesus,*
> *Happy I shall be;*
> *He is gently calling*
> *Little ones like me.*

What a contrast with the following by Alexander Mack Jr.

> *When the winds of misfortune roar*
> *And the waves of the sea are boisterous,*
> *Then contentment comforts thee.*
> *God, by His holy will, can give again*
> *The life that death has claimed.*
> *This is indeed divine salvation.*[136]

Hymn tunes are printed always in capitals and named often for a person or place in a composer's experience, or even the character of the hymn with which the tune is wedded: for example, in the 1879 hymnal are found such J. C. Ewing tunes as JUNIATA for Hymn 58 *("Songs of Praise the Angels Sing")*; HUNTINGDON at Hymn 769 *("Christian, the Morn Breaks Sweetly O'er Thee")*; and MEYERSDALE for Hymn 133 *("The Light of Sabbath Eve")*, named after that Pennsylvania town where Ewing conducted singing classes. In PART I of the 1884 *Brethren Hymnody* is included MONCE for Hymn 153 *("When Shall the Voice of Singing")*, a tune which bears his wife's maiden name.

---

[136] Heckman, *The Religious Poetry of Alexander Mack Jr.*, 44.

One of Ewing's more successful tunes, found in Part II of *Brethren Hymnody*, BAPTISMAL HYMN, was set to *"Following Jesus, Our Mighty Examplar"* (Hymn 267) by Mrs. C. L. Shacklock, of whom little is known. This is a more lengthy entry of stanza and chorus, with expressions typical of Brethren piety. The first stanza and chorus read:

Stanza One

> *Following Jesus, our mighty Exemplar,*
> *Ever obeying His blessed command,*
> *Even like Him at the river of Jordon,*
> *Now by the waters of cleansing we stand.*

Chorus

> *Buried with Christ, in His mission believing,*
> *Dying to sin, we are living again;*
> *Buried with Christ, and the Spirit receiving,*
> *Heirs of the Kingdom, with Him we shall reign.*

J. C. Ewing spent most of his career as a public school music teacher. He was Music Supervisor for the Lebanon, Ohio schools, a position he resigned in order to devote more time to preparing the 1884 hymnal. Also, he served as the first music teacher for the South Bend, Indiana public schools, and was a member of the South Bend Brethren Church. Elder H. R. Holsinger reported in the March 16, 1887 issue of *The Brethren Evangelist*:

> I am happy to report that we have a very pleasant little congregation here. We are not many in number, but I believe that we have as large a percentage of working members as any church in the state. We have preaching every Sunday morning at 11a.m. and 7 p.m., and a Sunday school at 10 and song service at 6:45p.m. Bro. J. C. Ewing conducts the latter, and leads all our music,

> and he does it well. I don't believe that any pastor in the ministry in the country has a better right hand man than I have in Bro. Ewing. We had a business meeting a few weeks ago, at which he was ordained to the office of Deacon, to which he had been called last fall. He had previously been elected to the ministry, but was not installed, and has never felt quite willing to accept that calling, but has now accepted the duties of the deacon. These were defined to him at the time of this installation, to embrace an active interest in and oversight of all the secular affairs of the church, and assisting the pastor in spiritual work and taking charge of meetings for worship in the absence of the pastor; with full privilege to preach when the spirit moves, and such other duties as the gospel may demand.[137]

Years later upon his death, the following obituary was recorded.

> Ewing, Bro. John C., a most highly respected, and the oldest member of the [First Brethren] Dayton Church, passed away on October 29th at the age of 88 years, 5 months, and 21 days. Bro. Ewing was the first Sunday school Superintendent and the first Choir Director of the Church. He had been a Deacon for many years. He was most influential in the establishment of the Dayton Church. Bro. Ewing rendered great service to the denomination. He was one of the leaders of the First Conference in Dayton in 1883. At the instructions of that conference he presented to the denomination its first hymn book in 1884. It was called *The Brethren Hymnody*. Two hymns of his own music from that were used in the funeral service.[138]

---

[137] *The Brethren Evangelist* (March 16, 1887, Volume IX, Number 11), 1.

[138] *The Brethren Evangelist* (January 22, 1938, Vol. LX, No. 4), 16. Regarding the date of Ewing's death, Wm. Beery, in *John Cook Ewing (1849–1937)* indicated

J. C. Ewing's significance cannot be overstated. This faithful, humble, hard-working servant of God was a very competent musician, and he composed an occasional hymn tune of merit. Ewing was the pioneer Brethren musician who paved the way for future hymnic production, particularly in the years ahead in the Church of the Brethren. One of his main accomplishments was certainly being a suitable teacher and mentor for William Beery, who contributed many years of fruitful music ministry, including prolific hymn tune composition, in the Church of the Brethren.

The Brethren Church also produced a modest sized collection, *Hymns of Worship and Songs of the Gospel* (1909), which contained traditional hymns and many gospel songs, with twenty-seven gospel hymns by C. Austin Miles (1868–1946) and sixteen by J. Lincoln Hall (1866–1930). Since that publication, however, there have been no further hymn books produced by The Brethren Church or the Fellowship of Grace Brethren Churches (begun in 1939). Through the twentieth century, congregations in both groups used a variety of nondenominational, evangelical hymnals.[139]

As mentioned above, the Old German Baptist Brethren continued to reprint their words-only 1882 hymnbook. The Dunkard Brethren (since 1926), an off-shoot of the Church of the Brethren, have utilized *The Brethren Hymnal* (1901), described below, as their official hymn book. Gospel songs are sung in both groups during their Sunday evening gatherings, at scheduled hymn singing, and in their homes.[140]

---

the 27th. However, upon investigation the obituary record given in *The Brethren Evangelist* is correct.

[139] Hedwig R. Durnbaugh and Nevin W. Fisher, "Gospel Songs," *The Brethren Encyclopedia*, Vol. 1, 560–561.

[140] For further discussion of the worship and hymn singing practices of the Old German Baptist Brethren and the Dunkard Brethren, see the following articles in

The remainder of this study of the spiritual themes in Brethren hymnody refers primarily to the hymnbook publications, hymn text authors and hymn tune composers of the Church of the Brethren.

The Brethren's Sunday School Song Book (1894) William Beery (1852–1956) and Other Composers

A call by progressives in the Church of the Brethren for collections of hymns and songs which would service those desiring the more energetic song literature popular in other Christian communities, and which would target specifically congregational singing by youth in Sunday school and for the advancement of the cause of missions, led to the publication of several "song" books which served to energize the Brethren in this new era of life and service. For example, the Brethren in the Lancaster, Pennsylvania area produced in 1879 *A Collection of Hymns for Sunday Schools and Public and Private Devotion.* Of the 318 hymns in this words-only collection, many were of the gospel song genre. Officially, however, the denomination had not authorized such a hymnbook.

In 1893 at the Annual Meeting, there was discussion regarding the usefulness of the current hymnal, and the old way of "lining" hymns was gradually being replaced with singing by reading musical notation. Being cautious about changing tradition too quickly, it was decided to keep the 1867 hymnal for Sunday morning worship, and they authorized the production of a songbook for other occasions and purposes. *The Brethren's Sunday School Song Book, for use in Sunday Schools , Prayer and Social Meetings* (1894) was compiled by William Beery and published by the Brethren's Publishing Company at Mount

---

The Brethren Encyclopedia: "Gospel Music" and "Gospel Songs" in Vol. 1, 559–561, "Worship, Public" in Vol. 2, 1373–1379, and "Worship" in Vol. 4, 2266–2267.

Morris, IL. The 185 hymns, set in shape notes, were prefaced by six pages of the rudiments of music. The song book contained mostly gospel hymns, including six tunes by J. Henry Showalter (1864–1947), six by George B. Holsinger (1857–1908), and twenty-five by William Berry. For three of the hymns, Beery wrote both text and tune. William Beery's wife, Adaline H. Beery (1859–1929), authored the hymn texts for thirteen hymns and composed both text and tune for four.

William Beery, mentioned previously as a student of J. C. Ewing's at Huntingdon Normal School (later Juniata College), followed in his teacher's footsteps as music instructor for the school (1878–1885) and later served as chair of the music department (1888–1908). He assisted in the compilation of the 1901 and 1925 Brethren hymnals, and edited several song books, including *Gospel Chimes for Sunday Schools and Religious Meetings* (1889) which included 110 hymns and was published by the Brethren's Publishing Company, Huntingdon, PA, and at Mount Morris, IL. In 1942 Beery wrote the historical sketch of his mentor cited above.[141] His last hymn tune, ELGIN, was composed in 1948 at age ninety-six for the hymn text *"I Will Not Be Afraid"* by G. E. M. Govan. Part of the tune's interest is that it begins in F minor and concludes in F major. The point is well-taken.

Gertrude A. Flory (1862–1930) authored four texts. Appearing for the first time in *The Brethren's Sunday School Song Book* was *"Take My Hand and Lead Me, Father,"* for which William Beery composed the tune, named many years later as HUNTINGDON. The hymn was carried over into all future Brethren hymnals. While in *The Brethren's Sunday School Song Book* (1894), *The Brethren Hymnal* (1901), and in *Hymnal: Church of the Brethren* (1925) Flory is not mentioned as the author, she is credited in *The Brethren Hymnal* (1951)

---

[141] William Beery and Peter E. Roussakis, *John Cook Ewing (1849–1937)*.

and in *Hymnal: A Worship Book* (1992). The match of Flory's text and Wm. Beery's tune "clicked" and made the hymn a favorite. From a Brethren point of view, it is readily seen why Mrs. Flory's hymn text received the response it deserved, capturing both the early "pilgrim" and the later "joyful hope" Brethren themes. That is consolidation. All three stanzas from the 1894 song book are given here.

> *Take my hand and lead me, Father,*
> *Through life's stormy pilgrimage;*
> *Let Thy light shine brighter, Father,*
> *On its dark, mysterious page;*
> *For I find my feet oft straying*
> *From the path of truth and right,*
> *Feel the need of Thy protection,*
> *And Thy light to shine more bright.*
>
> *For the road is rough and stony,*
> *And I cannot see my way;*
> *Yet, if Thou wilt deign to guide me*
> *With Thine own resplendent ray,*
> *I can never, never stumble,*
> *But shall walk close to Thy side,*
> *With a love so pure and trusting*
> *That no sin can e'er divide.*
>
> *Hold my hand in Thine, O Father,*
> *Till I reach the pearly gates;*
> *There I'll leave my cross and burden,*
> *For my star-gemmed crown awaits;*
> *Then I'll sing in strains of rapture,*
> *In the light of perfect day,*
> *Thou didst deign to guide me, Father,*
> *And hast led me all the way.*

In the 1894 song book and *The Brethren Hymnal* (1901) there was a chorus following each stanza of this hymn. While the 1925 and 1951 Brethren hymnals did not include the chorus, it did return in the 1992 hymnal.

All three of the composers mentioned above were prolific in their hymn tune composing, and served to energize the Brethren at that time. John Henry Showalter traveled widely, teaching in singing schools, in special Normal schools of music, and teaching singing in many Brethren congregations.[142] He was the editor of a collection entitled *Kingdom Songs: For Sunday School, Prayer Meeting, Christian Workers' Societies, and All Seasons of Praise* (Published by Authority of the General Mission Board. Elgin, IL: Brethren Publishing House, 1911). The second volume, *Kingdom Songs No. 2* published in 1918, was widely used in the Church of the Brethren.[143]

George B. Holsinger was a song leader, music teacher and composer. He taught piano, organ, choral music, harmony, and the history of music. He was the founder and chairman of the Music Department at the Virginia Normal School (later Bridgewater College) from 1882–1898. Holsinger produced *Gospel Songs and Hymns, No.1 For the Sunday School, Prayer Meeting, Social Meeting, General Song Service* (1898); *Songs of Praises* (Brethren Publishing House, 1906); and *Practical Exercises in Music Reading For Sunday Schools, Day Schools, Institutes and Normals* (Brethren Publishing House, 1908). He

---

[142] Dennis D. Martin and Elgin S. Moyer, "Showalter, John Henry," *The Brethren Encyclopedia*, Vol. 2, 1179.

[143] Roger E. Sappington, *The Brethren in Industrial America: A Source Book on the Development of the Church of the Brethren*, 1865–1915 (Elgin, IL: Brethren Press, 1985), 282–283.

served as chief editor for *The Brethren Hymnal* (1901), and held singing classes in many Brethren congregations.[144]

The publication of these ancillary song books was a tangible indication of "how the times they had been a changin'" in Brethren church life, worship, and congregational singing.

The Brethren Hymnal (1901)

By the turn of the century in a great number of congregations, *The Brethren's Sunday School Song Book* had replaced the words-only 1867 hymnal and the 1879 *Brethren's Tune and Hymn Book* as their main collection of hymns and songs used in worship. In addition, at the 1900 Annual Meeting it was reported that leading congregations had adopted non-Brethren hymnbooks.[145] It was decided that a new hymnbook should be produced which may service all of the people's song preferences. George B. Holsinger, J. Henry Showalter, and William Beery served as the Music Committee, while D. L. Miller (1841–1921), L. T. Holsinger (1850–1937), and H. B. Brumbaugh (1836–1919) comprised the Hymn [Text] Committee. A year later, *The Brethren Hymnal: A Collection of Psalms, Hymns and Spiritual Songs: Suited for Song Service in Christian Worship, for Church Service, Social Meetings and Sunday Schools* was published. A word-only edition and an edition with shape-note musical notation were published. The edition with musical notation became affectionately referred to as the "Old Black Book." The next two main hymnals of the Church of the Brethren in the twentieth century would be nicknamed also by the color of their covers.

---

[144] Nevin W. Fisher, "Holsinger, George Blackburn," *The Brethren Encyclopedia*, Vol. 1, 621.

[145] Bowman provides discussion of the thinking, circumstances, and trends which led to the publication of the 1894 *Song Book* and the 1901 hymnal. *Brethren Society*, 161–163.

Of the 742 entries, a section was included with seventy-five Sunday school, prayer meeting, and evangelistic hymns. The hymnbook contained a Scripture Index; an Index of Subjects; an Index of Authors and their Hymns, which included brief accounts of information about each writer; an Index of Composers and Their Tunes, with information about each composer as well; a Metrical Index of Tunes; an Alphabetical Index of Tunes; and an Index of First Lines. From the standpoint of these indices alone, this was an impressive production.

Some of the well-known authors and the number of hymns included in this thoroughly Anglo-American hymnal were:

> William Cullen Bryant (1794–1878): American Unitarian, 2
> William Cowper (1731–1800): Church of England, 6
> Fanny Crosby (1823–1915): Methodist, 8
> Philip Doddridge (1702–1751): English Congregationalist, 15
> John Fawcett (1740–1817): English Baptist, 4
> Oliver Wendell Holmes (1809–1894): American Unitarian, 1
> James Montgomery (1771–1854): English Moravian, 15
> John Newton (1725–1807): Church of England, 22
> Isaac Watts (1674–1748): English Congregationalist, 81
> Elder John Walter Wayland (1872–1962): Church of the Brethren, 5 (two for which he composed the music)
> Charles Wesley (1708–1788): Church of England, 37.

Except for the last printing of *Ein Sammlung* in 1903, we may say with assurance that with the publication and use of *The Brethren Hymnal* (1901), there were no longer two tracks of Brethren hymnody as there were in the nineteenth century. With that shift completed, Hedda Durnbaugh laments that, "the Brethren have lost their German heritage and, along with it, the type of piety and spirituality that the hymns reflect."[146] In her analysis, Durnbaugh explained the twentieth century progression of the two-fold loss:

> First, along with the hymns, a source for private and individual devotion, spiritual nurture, and strengthening of the faith was lost. This was all the more difficult to replace, because after the demise of German hymnal-printing for the Brethren, text-only hymnals, which had served for reading as much as for singing, were no longer published. Thus, and along with the hymns the acknowledgement of the vitality to meet the spiritual needs of the individual through hymns was forgotten over time.[147]

However, while the piety of the German hymnody of the Brethren ceased to be a dominant part of Brethren spirituality, distinctives of classic Brethren spirituality remained and continued to be practiced and expressed. An example from *The Brethren Hymnal* (1901) is a hymn text by S. M. Hoover. Stanzas one and two of *"The Pilgrim's Parting Hymn,"* based on Revelation 21:3, are given below. The pilgrim theme from the piety of the past is melded with the idea of the heavenward joy which dominated the text writing and tune composing of this Energizing era.

> *"Now, pilgrims, let us go in peace"*
> *While through this world we rove;*
> *Till all these parting moments cease,*
> *And we shall meet above.*
> *Though trials here our souls annoy,*
> *And foes beset the road,*
> *We're hast'ning to eternal joy,*
> *Where we shall rest with God.*

---

[146] H. T. Durnbaugh, "Changes Reflected in Brethren Hymnody," 200.
[147] Ibid., 201.

> *Let us rejoice in God our King,*
> *While pilgrims here we rove;*
> *And join with heart and voice to sing*
> *The wonders of his love.*
> *Soon we shall reach the heav'nly land,*
> *And tread the peaceful shore;*
> *And there unite, a glorious band,*
> *Our Jesus to adore.*

Also, stanza two of Hymn 387 (author not given) says:

> *A pilgrimage my lot,*
> *My home is in the skies;*
> *I nightly pitch my tent below,*
> *And daily higher rise.*

Worthy of note are two hymns by Brethren Elder John Walter Wayland (1872–1962). He was also an instructor at Madison State College, Harrisonburg, Virginia, and a writer of widely used history texts.[148] *"If I Your Lord have Washed Your Feet"* (Hymn 247, for which George B. Holsinger composed the tune ELGIN), and *"Know Ye What I have Done to You"* (Hymn 252, headed in the hymnal as *"Love Makes Humble Service Sweet,"* and for which Wayland also composed the tune), speak to the ordinance of feet-washing. The four stanzas of the first are given here.

> *"If I your Lord have washed your feet,*
> *Ye also ought the same to do;*
> *For in your service it is meet*
> *To do as I have done to you."*

---

[148] Wm. Beery, *Brethren Hymns, Hymnals, Authors and Composers*, 10; and Francis F. Wayland, "Wayland, John Walter," *The Brethren Encyclopedia*, Vol. 2, 1323.

> *To all his loved ones here below*
> *This plain command the Lord has giv'n;*
> *And by obedience we may show*
> *Our love for Him who is in Heaven.*
>
> *How happy is the man who knows*
> *That Jesus served with His own hands!*
> *Thrice happy is the man who shows*
> *Obedience to the Lord's commands!*
>
> *In humble service we shall please*
> *The Author of the Living Word;*
> *For as we serve the least of these*
> *His brethren, we shall serve the Lord.*

Other Brethren hymn authors represented in the hymnal include Adaline Beery, 6; Sallie Kagey Holsinger, wife of composer George B. Holsinger, 3; Elder James A. Sell (1845–1948), 2; Gertrude A. Flory, 1; and 1 by Elder Albert Cassel Wieand (1871–1954), co-founder and president of Bethany Theological Seminary. Wieand's hymn, "On the Radiant Threshold" (Hymn 76), represents the kind of "churchly" hymn text favored increasingly by Brethren hymnal compilers in the twentieth century. Stanza one of his hymn for The Lord's Day reads:

> *On the radiant threshold*
> *Of this dawning day,*
> *In the sacred stillness,*
> *We will pause and pray.*
> *In the morning, noon, and evening,*
> *We would seek Thy side;*
> *O do Thou, dear Lord, befriend us,*
> *O be Thou our guide.*

Both standard style and gospel song tunes are represented in the hymnal. The Index of Composers contains a "Who's Who" of American church musicians:

>Philip Bliss (1833–1876): 4
>William Bradbury (1816–1868): 19
>Jeremiah Ingalls (1764–1828): 4
>Edmund S. Lorenz (1854–1942): 1
>Robert Lowry (1829–1899): 3
>Lowell Mason (1792–1872): 49.

In the hymnal there were a great number of tunes by the "big three" Brethren composers. Selected tune names of special interest to Brethren are mentioned here.

William Beery: 10 tunes; his tune for Hymn 248, a hymn on feet-washing, text by Adaline H. Beery, was named LOWLY SERVICE.

George B. Holsinger: 58 tunes; his tune for Hymn 107 was named QUINTER; the tune for Hymn 247, Wayland's hymn on feet-washing, was named ELGIN; and his tune for Hymn 249, another hymn on feet-washing, was named OBEDIENCE.

J. Henry Showalter: 45 tunes.

Other tunes by Brethren composers included one at Hymn 169 by Elder Daniel Medford Click (1858–1947), and one for Hymn 232 by Elder Galen B. Royer (1862–1951), a college administrator in Valparaiso, Indiana.

It became common for the Brethren musicians to offer special training sessions for the church music education of parishioners. In addition, William Beery in 1899 offered a series of articles in the denominational magazine, *The Gospel Messenger*, making several suggestions for the effective planning and conduct of song services. For example, remarks were directed to the minister regarding hymn selection; to song leaders, that they establish appropriate tempos; and to the persons in the pews with respect to adhering to the notation of the music given in the hymnal or song book, and following the song leader.[149]

Although most Brethren authors and composers are not listed in the indices, it is clear Holsinger and Showalter were having a great old time! They loved to compose hymn tunes, and they wanted Brethren to have a rousing, joyful, uplifting Christian experience. Through their composing, teaching, and leading music, Brethren musicians served to energize the life and work of Brethren Christians individually and as a denomination during this period of adjustment and progress.

---

[149] William Beery's series of articles on the "Song Service in the Sanctuary" appeared in 1899 in three issues of the *Gospel Messenger* (Part I, February 4; Part II, February 11; Part III, February 18).

The large selection of hymns and worship resources in the [1951] *Brethren Hymnal* indicates the ecumenical nature of contemporary Brethren worship, for the present hymnal is replete with social-gospel hymns, classical hymns of Protestantism, gospel songs from revivalism, and older and newer selections from Brethren authors and composers.

Donald F. Durnbaugh

Evolving: Early 20th Century to 1958

Following what we've referred to as the Energizing era of Brethren hymnody with its revivalist piety and gospel songs, many congregations in the Church of the Brethren, as well as in The Brethren Church, practiced all of the "innovations" which caused so much controversy from the 1850s to the 1880s: instruments in the sanctuary, missions activities, higher education, evangelistic efforts, Sunday schools, Bible studies and prayer meetings. Dennis D. Martin commented:

> Early in the 20th century such leaders as [A. C.] Wieand (CB), C. C. Ellis (CB), [J. C.] Cassel (BC, FGBC), and [C. F.] Yoder (BC), were especially open to the pursuit of spiritual 'empowerment' and 'complete sanctification' along the lines of the Keswick Convention and related movements. Family worship, once wide-spread among Brethren, gave way increasingly in the 20th century to private devotional exercises.[150]

All of these innovations were viewed in the Church of the Brethren as vehicles for enabling "spiritual empowerment." And yet, there were still objections raised, especially regarding musical instruments. An editorial in 1908 in the denominational magazine, *The Gospel Messenger*, stated emphatically that "the brass band belongs to the world and has no fit place in any of our religious services.... Instead of giving way to the popular influence, we need to study, more closely than ever before, the spirit and simplicity of New Testament worship."[151] Again in 1919, questions were raised and debated regarding a number of issues, including the matter of musical instruments in worship. In 1920 the conservatives' effort to ban officially the use of

---

[150] Dennis D. Martin, "Spiritual Life," *The Brethren Encyclopedia*, Vol 2, 1210.
[151] Kenneth I. Morse, "Worship, Public," *The Brethren Encyclopedia*, Vol. 2, 1377.

instruments was voted down.[152] Nevin Fisher explained: "After 1900 change was more difficult to resist. Sometimes pianos and organs were installed or 'set in' meetinghouses for special occasions such as weddings and youth programs."[153] As the 1920s drew to a close, three-fourths of all Brethren congregations had musical instruments, and one-fourth had organized choirs, one purpose of which was to support congregational singing.[154]

Hymnal: Church of the Brethren (1925)

It was clear that the Brethren were evolving; that is, they were maturing, progressing, developing, not only in theological debate, but also in their hymnic activities. Even in the midst of the controversies over liberalism on the one hand and fundamentalism on the other, the Church of the Brethren managed to produce a hymnal (the "blue" book) in 1925 which would serve them for the next quarter of a century and help steady the spiritual ship. What kind of piety did the hymns in this hymnbook express?

The committee for *Hymnal: Church of the Brethren* (1925) was chaired by J. S. Flory with William Beery serving as the chief music consultant. This was the first Brethren hymnal which was produced in two musical editions, one with round notes and one with shape notation. Also for the first time, the 1925 hymnal contained several kinds of service music and worship aids: musical responses for church choirs, a section of responsive readings of scripture, printed prayers, choral or spoken offertories and benedictions, hymns for opening of worship and

---

[152] An account of the query, the debate and the responses are given in Bowman, *Brethren Society*, 273–283.

[153] Nevin W. Fisher, "Musical Instruments," *The Brethren Encyclopedia,* Vol. 2, 900.

[154] Bowman, *Brethren Society*, 257.

hymns for closing. All these worship aids indicated a growing trend toward more formal worship services, far different from that of the basic Singing-Praying-Preaching-Explaining practice of the early Brethren.

Of the 484 hymns, a significant number were authored or composed by Brethren. They are given below, followed by the location of their inclusion in other Brethren hymnbooks: SSSB refers to *The Brethren's Sunday School Song Book* (1894); BH'01 refers to *The Brethren Hymnal* (1901); BH '51 stands for *The Brethren Hymnal* (1951); and HWB indicates *Hymnal: A Worship Book* (1992). Brethren authors included:

> Adaline H. Beery (1859–1929): Hymn 71, "Hail, Blessed Trinity" (Text & Tune) [SSSB 115]; Hymn 256, "Lo, a Gleam from Yonder Heaven" (Tune: JUNIATA by Wm. Beery); [BH'51 454; HWB 591]
>
> Gertrude Flory (1862–1930): Hymn 254, "Take My Hand and Lead Me, Father" (Tune: HUNTINGDON by Wm. Beery) [SSSB 135, BH'51 298; HWB 601]
>
> Marguerite Bixler Garrett (1871–1963): Hymn 53, "Hear, O Hear Us, Heavenly Father" (Text & Tune); Hymn 308, "Brother, Here's a Message" (Text & Tune)
>
> Edyth Hillery Hay (1891–1943): Hymn 13, "Lord, With Devotion We Pray" (Text & Tune) [BH'51, 456; HWB 79]; Hymn 122, "He Loveth Me" (Credited as the author; however, Wm. Beery listed her as composer in his booklet, Brethren Hymns, Hymnals, Authors and Composers)
>
> John W. Wayland (1872–1952): Hymn 206, "Gracious King Enthroned Above" [BH'01, 62]
>
> Albert Cassel Wieand (1871–1954): Hymn 18, "On the Radiant Threshold" [BH'01, 76; BH'51, 65; HWB 649]

Mary Stoner Wine (1885–1959): Hymn 307, ""Peace, Perfect Peace Have They."[155]

Once again we must highlight Elder John W. Wayland. Straightforward, the quality of his poetry stands out, the theology clear and true, and in this case a prayer hymn for coming to Christ and growing in him, a hymn of invitation and dedication, a hymn for all pious Christians, exuding the devotion of the author, and with a timeless Brethren theme. The four stanzas of Hymn 206 read:

> *Gracious King enthroned above,*
> *I would come to Thee;*
> *Longing for Thy smile of love,*
> *Lord, I come to Thee.*
> *Help of all our helpless race,*
> *All our hope is in Thy grace;*
> *Show to me Thy smiling face,*
> *Lord, I come to Thee.*
>
> *In the merit of Thy Son,*
> *Lord, I come to Thee;*
> *Christ for me has favor won,*
> *Lord, I come to Thee.*
> *Let me now be reconciled,*
> *Though a wand'rer from the wild;*
> *O receive me as a child,*
> *Lord, I come to Thee.*
>
> *With the Spirit for my guide,*
> *Lord, I come to Thee.*
> *All myself in Thee to hide,*

---

[155] A complete listing of Brethren authors and composers in the 1925 hymnal is given in Wm. Beery's booklet, *Brethren Hymns, Hymnals, Authors and Composers*.

Lord, I come to Thee.
Cares unbidden fill my breast;
Sorrow has my soul oppressed;
Give a fainting pilgrim rest,
Lord, I come to Thee.

Wash me in the cleansing flood,
Lord, I come to Thee.
Make me [pure] in Jesus' blood,
Lord, I come to Thee.
Lord of love, bid sorrow cease;
Source of joy, my joy increase;
Father, fill my soul with peace,
For I come to Thee.

The authors with the most texts in the 1925 hymnal include: Isaac Watts (1674–1748), 23; Charles Wesley (1707–1788), 23; Fanny Crosby (1820–1915), 13; and James Montgomery (1771–1854), 11. In the 1867 Brethren hymnbook were included twenty of Montgomery's hymns. Why did Brethren sing so many hymns by James Montgomery? They are worth considering because they reflect themes to which Brethren gave attention, and they say much about the devotional fabric of the Brethren before and during this time.

James Montgomery (1771–1854)

Montgomery was a Scottish Moravian. His adult years included his holding a job as a clerk in a bookshop. In answer to a want ad he secured a job for a radical weekly newspaper in Sheffield, England. When the editor was forced to leave England for fear of persecution for his political articles, Montgomery became owner of the paper and continued producing the *Sheffield Register* (renamed the *Iris* by Montgomery) for three years. On two occasions he was jailed for seditious libel. In prison he wrote poetry. In 1825 he discontinued the paper and devoted the rest of his life to literary and philanthropic pursuits. He continued to write poetry and lectured about it. At one point he was named First Citizen of Sheffield.

James Montgomery's non-hymnic poetry has not been regarded as especially note-worthy. The total output of hymns, numbering 400 however, is for what he is most remembered and endeared. Albert Edward Bailey (1871–1951) said of Montgomery:

> One cannot call him a great poet, but he knew how to express with sincerity, fervor, simplicity and beauty the emotions and aspirations of the common Christian. Out of his work we might almost construct a definition of a hymn: *religious verse that expresses the spiritual life* in forms of beauty suitable for worship. In the primary background for his hymn-writing lies his piety ... Montgomery said of his Moravian upbringing: "Whatever we did was done in the name and for the sake of Jesus Christ, whom we were taught to regard in the amiable and endearing light of a friend and brother."[156]

The eleven hymns by Montgomery in *Hymnal: Church of the Brethren* (1925) include: "Prayer is the Soul's Sincere Desire" Hymn 47; "Bless the Lord, My Soul" Hymn 50; "To Thy Temple We Repair" Hymn 59; "Angels From the Realms of Glory" Hymn 108; "Go to Dark Gethsemane" Hymn 134; "The Lord is My Shepherd" Hymn 260; "In the Hour of Trial" Hymn 321; "Hosanna Be the Children's Song" Hymn 401; "The God of

---

[156] Albert Edward Bailey, *The Gospel in Hymns: Backgrounds and Interpretations* (New York: Charles Scribner's Sons, 1950), 156. Bailey was Director of Religious Education at the Worcester Academy in Massachusetts, and wrote numerous books on the subject of religion and the arts.

Harvest Praise" Hymn 422; "Pour Out Thy Spirit from on High" Hymn 446; "According to Thy Gracious Word" Hymn 466.

A sampling here of his hymn texts include stanzas one and four of *"Prayer is the Soul's Sincere Desire."*

> *Prayer is the soul's sincere desire.*
> *Unuttered or expressed;*
> *The motion of a hidden fire*
> *That trembles in the breast.*

> *O Thou, by whom we come to God,*
> *The Life, the Truth, the Way!*
> *The path of prayer Thyself hast trod;*
> *Lord, teach us how to pray.*

Stanzas one and three of "In the Hour of Trial" read:

> *In the hour of trial,*
> *Jesus plead for me,*
> *Lest by base denial,*
> *I depart from Thee;*
> *When Thou see'st me waver,*
> *With a look recall,*
> *Nor, for fear or favor,*
> *Suffer me to fall.*

> *Should Thy mercy send me*
> *Sorrow, toil, and woe;*
> *Or should pain attend me*
> *On my path below;*
> *Grant that I may never*
> *Fail Thy hand to see;*
> *Grant that I may ever*
> *Cast my care on Thee.*

Hymn 304 in the 1925 hymnbook was by Paul Gerhardt (1607–1676), a favorite hymn writer of the Brethren in the Emerging era of Brethren history and hymnody. The hymn, *"Give to the Winds Thy Fears,"* was also among the twelve of his included in *Das Kleine Davidische Psalterspiel* (1744). The five stanzas as translated by John Wesley (1703–1791) are the following:

> *Give to the winds thy fears;*
> *Hope, and be undismayed;*
> *God hears thy sighs and counts thy tears,*
> *God shall lift up thy head.*
>
> *Still heavy is thy heart?*
> *Still sink thy spirits down?*
> *Cast off the weight, let fear depart,*
> *And ev'ry care be gone.*
>
> *Commit thou all thy griefs*
> *And ways into His hands,*
> *To His sure truth and tender care,*
> *Who earth and heaven commands.*
>
> *Who points the clouds their course,*
> *Whom winds and seas obey,*
> *He shall direct thy wand'ring feet,*
> *He shall prepare the way.*
>
> *Leave to His sov'reign will*
> *To choose and to command:*
> *With wonder filled, thou then shalt own*
> *How wise, how strong His hand.*

Broad Spectrum of Inclusions: Evolving Spirituality

Hymn texts and tunes from a wide spectrum of traditions represented in the Church of the Brethren an acculturation and assimilation of the broader culture of church music in America. To make the point, other selected authors and translators in the hymnal include the following:

> Cecil Francis Alexander (1834–1895)
> The Venerable Bede (673–735)
> Louis F. Benson (1855–1930)
> Bernard of Clairvaux (1091–1153)
> Bernard of Cluny (12th c.)
> William Cullen Bryant (1794–1878)
> Clement of Alexandria (c. 170–220)
> William Cowper (1731–1800)
> Fanny Crosby (1820–1915)
> William Chatterton Dix (1837–1898)
> Timothy Dwight (1752–1817)
> Charlotte Eliot (1789–1871)
> Paul Gerhardt (1606–1676)
> Johann Wolfgang von Goethe (1749–1832)
> Reginald Heber (1793–1826)
> Oliver Wendell Holmes (1809–1894)
> Thomas Ken (1637–1711)
> Rudyard Kipling (1865–1936)
> Samuel W. Longfellow (1819–1892)
> William Pearson Merrill (1867–1954)
> John Mason Neal (1818–1866)
> John Henry Newman (1801–1890)
> Frank Mason North (1850–1935)
> Ray Palmer (1808–1887).

An example of a hymn which indicates the Church of the Brethren's movement toward "mainline-ism" in hymnody is a text by Ray Palmer, American Congregationalist (incorrectly described as Presbyterian in BH '01). Palmer made a commitment to ministry at the evangelical Park Street Church in Boston. He served for fifteen years at the Congregational Church in Bath, Maine. Stanzas one and three of Hymn 270 read:

> *My faith looks up to Thee,*
> *Thou Lamb of Calvary,*
> *Savior divine!*
> *Now hear me while I pray,*
> *Take all my guilt away,*
> *Oh, let me from this day*
> *Be wholly Thine.*
>
> *While life's dark maze I tread,*
> *And griefs around me spread,*
> *Be Thou my guide;*
> *Bid darkness turn to day,*
> *Wipe sorrow's tears away,*
> *Nor let me ever stray*
> *From Thee aside.*

Two other examples from *Hymnal: Church of the Brethren* (1925) reveal other aspects of the evolving spirituality of some Brethren during this theologically controversial period. The first is a hymn authored by William Pierson Merrill (1867–1954), an American Presbyterian educated at Union Theological Seminary in New York City. He served in churches in Philadelphia, Chicago, then at Brick Presbyterian Church in New York City. He was an author on subjects pertaining to liberalism, in particular "world brotherhood by the Christian spirit and ideals."[157] Hymn 36, his *"Rise Up, O Men of God,"* is included in the section of the hymnal for "World Peace and Brotherhood," a worthy desire especially during the aftermath of

---

[157] Bailey, *The Gospel in Hymns*, 572.

World War I, and certainly in line with the Brethren positions of getting along with others and of non-resistance. The 1911 Annual Meeting had formed a Peace Committee to assist conscientious objectors and to distribute peace literature.[158] The hymn begins:

> *Rise up, O men of God!*
> *Have done with lesser things.*
> *Give heart and soul and mind and strength*
> *To serve the King of Kings.*

Bailey suggests "lesser things may refer to church suppers, entertainments, bowling teams or whatever activities only vaguely suggest the objects of Christian living. All energies of the soul must be devoted to implementing the rule of God in human society"[159] Lesser things may be thought of as synonymous with any reference to worldly things in eighteenth and nineteenth century Brethren writings. However, while in the eighteenth century hymns were directed toward the individual, here the focus is the corporate church. The Brethren were called in the nineteenth century to non-conformity with the world. Here the call may be not to conform to the ways of many other churches. Stanza two reads:

> *Rise up, O men of God!*
> *His kingdom tarries long:*
> *Bring in the day of brotherhood*
> *And end the night of wrong.*

A. E. Bailey's interpretation says: "Two thousand years of theological wrangling and the drive for power have only

---

[158] Stephen L. Longenecker, *The Brethren During the Age of World War: The Church of the Brethren Encounter with Modernism, 1914–1950* (Elgin, IL: Brethren Press, 2006), xxxii.

[159] Bailey, *The Gospel in Hymns*, 572.

postponed the kingdom of God [on earth]; the rule of God secured only by cultivating the attitude of brotherhood, for that alone will cure the ills of society."[160] This is the Social Gospel.

The other hymn is *"Where Cross the Crowded Ways of Life"* (Hymn 339) by Frank Mason North (1850–1935). He was educated at Wesleyan University in Connecticut, and served pastorates in the Methodist Episcopal Church. From 1916 to 1920 he served as president of the Federal Council of Churches of Christ in America. Stanzas one and four say:

> *Where cross the crowded ways of life,*
> *Where sound the cries of race and clan,*
> *Above the noise of selfish strife,*
> *We hear Thy voice, O Son of man!*
>
> *The cup of water given for Thee*
> *Still holds the freshness of Thy grace;*
> *Yet long these multitudes to see*
> *The sweet compassion of Thy face.*

Stephen L. Longenecker wrote of North's hymn: "Written in 1905, North's hymn applied faith to urban problems, a classic Social Gospel approach to what religious progressives considered one of the most perplexing problems of their era."[161] Indeed this was the case. Albert T. Ronk commented:

> Taking a wider view of the Brethren scene, the theology of the Fraternity did not suffer much until the turn of the twentieth century ... it was not until the Federal Council of Churches was formed in 1908, and became its stentorian voice, that liberal theology and the Social Gospel penetrated the Brethren shield.... Peace moves, prohibition, labor issues, new deal, social security, birth-

---

[160] Ibid.

[161] Longenecker, *The Brethren During the Age of World War*, 85.

> control, ad infinitum, were sponsored. This is not a criticism of the encouraged good, but the fact that the slogan was established of the Kingdom of God on earth.... It is relevant to these facts and time that a number of her most able ministers left the Brethren Church in the 1920s for the liberal pastures of Presbyterianism.[162]

In *Hymnal: Church of the Brethren* (1925) most Brethren hymn tune composers are all familiar names. For interest, the following listing also includes selected hymn titles, tune names, and the location of the text and tune in other Brethren hymn books.[163]

> William Berry (1852–1956): Hymn 170, "Come, Holy Ghost, In Love," Latin text, trans. by Ray Palmer; Hymn 183, "Blessed Bible, How I Love It," text from the 1867 Hymnbook; Hymn 254 "Take My Hand, And Lead Me, Father," tune: HUNTINGDON; text by Gertrude A. Flory (SSSB, 135; BH '01, 730; BH '51, 298; HWB, 601); Hymn 256, "Lo, A Gleam from Yonder Heaven," tune: JUNIATA; text by Adaline H. Berry (BH '01, 728; BH '51, 454; HWB, 591); Hymn 298, "My God, the Spring of All My Joys," text by Isaac Watts (SSSB, 1; BH '01, 446).
>
> Marguerite Bixler Garrett (1871–1963), who taught music at Mt. Morris College in Illinois and at Manchester College in Indiana: Hymn 53, "Hear, O Hear Us, Heavenly Father" (text and tune); Hymn 308, "Brother, Here's a Message" (text and tune).

---

[162] A. T. Ronk, *History of The Brethren Church*, 14–15.

[163] A complete listing of the Brethren hymn tune composers in the 1925 hymnal is given in Wm. Beery's booklet, *Brethren Hymns, Hymnals, Authors and Composers*, 3–5.

Edyth Hillery Hay (1891–1943): Hymn 13, "Lord, with Devotion We Pray" text and tune [BH '51, 456; HWB 79]; Hymn 122, "He Loveth Me" (credited in the hymnal as author, but listed as composer in Beery's booklet)[164]; Hymn 217, "The Way is Dark," text by John W. Lear (1870–1959), Brethren Pastor and Professor at Bethany Theological Seminary.

George B. Holsinger (1857–1908): Tunes for Hymns 137, 312, 379, 431.

J. Henry Showalter (1864–1947): Tunes for Hymns 60, 133, 216, 223, 228, 256, 268, 291, 294, 395, 376, 423, 451.

Seventy Gospel hymns were included in the 1925 hymnal, more than in any other hymnal of the Church of the Brethren. Other well-known non-Brethren Gospel tune composers represented in the hymnal include:

Philip Bliss (1838–1876): 6
William Bradbury (1816–1968): 16
William Howard Doane (1831–1915): 9
Charles H. Gabriel (1856–1932): 1
William Kirkpatrick (1838–1921): 6
Robert Lowry (1826–1899): 7.

In addition, the usage of tunes by many other highly regarded composers is also reflective of the Brethren hymnal committee's desire to demonstrate its knowledge of church music history and the broader usages current in America's denominations, and to help cultivate Brethren sensibilities among its people for the same. Examples of composers and their tunes include:

Sir Joseph Barnby (1838–1896): LONGWOOD for "Spirit of God, Descend Upon My Heart" (Hymn 174)

---

[164] Ibid., 4.

Ludwig van Beethoven (1770–1837): HYMN TO JOY for "Joyful, Joyful, We Adore Thee" (91)

Louis Bourgeois (1500–1565): OLD HUNDREDTH for "Praise God From Whom All Blessings Flow" (497)

William Croft (1678–1727): ST. ANNE for "Our God, Our Help in Ages Past" (76) [listed again as the original wording]

John Bacchus Dykes (1823–1876): ST. AGNES for "Jesus, the Very Thought of Thee" (290)

George Frederic Handel (1685–1759): BRADFORD for "I Know that My Redeemer Lives" (163)

Franz Joseph Haydn (1737–1806): AUSTRIA for "Glorious Things of Thee are Spoken" (192)

Martin Luther (1483–1546): EIN' FESTE BURG for "A Mighty Fortress is Our God" (258)

Lowell Mason (1792–1872): AZMON for "O for a Thousand Tongues to Sing" (113)

Wolfgang Amadeus Mozart (1756–1791): ELLESDIE for "Jesus, I My Cross Have Taken" (235)

Samuel Sebastian Wesley (1810–1876): AURELIA for "The Church's One Foundation" (185).

All this is an indication, as far as hymn selection and compilation were concerned, that the Brethren hymnal committee members viewed their efforts as being in line with the larger church music practice in America. They valued that, and they desired that the Brethren at large value that as well, unfortunately to the exclusion at that point of almost all of the early Brethren hymnic heritage. Only two authors from the Emerging period were included: Paul Gerhardt for *"Give to the Winds Thy Fears"* (304) mentioned above, and Benjamin Schmolck (1672–1737) for *"My Jesus, As Thou Wilt"* (234).

In addition, no chorale harmonizations by Johann Sebastian Bach are present in the hymnal. There is no indication of meters and no metrical index. Evidently, according to Evelyn M. Frantz, "the concept of singing one hymn with one tune was so well ingrained that no one cared to investigate substitutes."[165] Some of that would change with the publication of *The Brethren Hymnal* (1951).

The Brethren Hymnal (1951)

During this Evolving era, tensions persisted between progressives and those who called for resistance to modernism and a restoration of traditional Brethren practices. In the 1930s a booklet was produced which outlined the positions of the conservatives.[166] They cited what they believed to be a laxity of faithfulness and a giving in to the tendencies of "worldlyism". For example, they stood in opposition to the general omission of the Lord's Prayer in worship, the disuse of the salutation of love (the Holy Kiss), the preaching of world and human brotherhood other than by evangelism, and the use of musical instruments in worship. It is not surprising, given the influence of liberal theology, that there would be a departure in 1926 of those who established themselves as Dunkard Brethren. In spite of this, as Stephen Longenecker records, "most conservatives remained within the fold, loyal to the denomination but upset over its direction."[167] Dennis Martin, summarizing the outward spiritual expressions of the Church of the Brethren in the 1940s, said: "much of the fervor formerly expressed in revival meetings, missions education, and the encouragement of daily devotional exercises was transferred to social action, peace testimony, and relief and service ventures."[168]

---

[165] Evelyn M. Frantz, "The Influence of American Music on Four Brethren Hymnals," *Brethren Life and Thought* Volume XX (Summer 1975): 173.
[166] Longenecker, *The Brethren During the Age of World War*, 200–203.
[167] Ibid., 200.
[168] Dennis D. Martin, "Spiritual Life," *The Brethren Encyclopedia*, 1210.

Innovations such as graded choirs, "higher" orders of worship, worship bulletins, baptisteries, and offerings to support the professional ministry and the denomination, were examples of the trend toward more formality in Brethren worship.[169] *The Brethren Hymnal* (1951) reflected and helped further these practices, all of which were congruent with those of many mainline Protestant churches.[170]

Nevin W. Fisher (BM, Eastman School of Music, 1940, and MM, Northwestern University, 1947), who taught at several Church of the Brethren colleges, served as Editor-in-Chief and Music Editor. The hymnal, which took six years of concentrated effort, was completed by committees on doctrine, music, literary quality, and worship values. Paul Minnich Robinson (b. 1914), President of Bethany Theological Seminary, chaired the worship committee. Alvin F. Brightbill (1903–1976), faculty member at Bethany Theological Seminary, conducted hymn festivals and workshops throughout the denomination to introduce the hymnal.

There are distinctive features of the hymnal, often referred to as the "red book". Included were twenty-nine German hymns in English translation. While this is less than five per cent of the 614 hymns in the hymnal, nevertheless, this was significant, for it demonstrated the committee valuing the need to keep in touch with the early Brethren heritage. Thirteen of these had appeared in previous German Brethren hymnals, and four were by Brethren authors whom we have cited previously. The four German Brethren authors were:

> Johannes Naas (1670–1741): "Savior of My Soul," Hymn 361 [HWB 549]
> Christopher Sauer Jr. (1721–1784): "Death, Where is Thy Sting," Hymn 418

---

[169] Longenecker, *The Brethren During the Age of World* War, 100, 102.
[170] D. Durnbaugh, *Fruit of the Vine*, 520.

Jakob Stoll (1731–1822): "Oh, How in the Time So Urgent," Hymn 428 [incorrectly attributed to Alexander Mack Sr.]

Alexander Mack Jr. (1712–1808): "Bless, O Lord, This Church of Thine," Hymn 493 [HWB 40, the order of the stanzas being altered].

Some of the other German heritage authors represented include:

Nikolaus Decius (c.1490–1541): "All Glory Be to God on High," Hymn 13

Paul Gerhardt (1607–1676): "All My Heart This Night Rejoices," Hymn 140; "O Sacred Head, Now Wounded," Hymn 168; and "O Jesus, Thy Boundless Love," Hymn 181.

Philipp Nicolai (1556–1608): "Wake, Awake, for Night is Flying," Hymn 207 [Tune: WACHET AUF]

Martin Rinkart (1586–1649): "Now Thank We All Our God," Hymn 601 [Tune: NUN DANKET by Johann Crüger (1598–1661), Harmonized by Felix Mendelssohn (1809–1847)]

Johann Schleffer (1624–1677): "Thee Will I Love," Hymn 118

Benjamin Schmolck (1672–1737): "My Jesus, As Thou Wilt," Hymn 360

Johann C. Schwedler (1672–1730): "Ask Ye What Great Thing I Know," Hymn 331

Christian Knorr von Rosenroth (1636–1689): "Jesus, Sun of Righteousness," Hymn 414 [Tune from Freylinghausen's Gesangbuch (1704)]

George Weissel (1590–1635): "LiftUp Your Heads," Hymn 203 [Tune from Klug's Gesangbuch (1535), Harmonized by J. S. Bach (1685–1750)].

Other Brethren authors and composers and their hymn texts and tunes of special merit, and which are reflections of the spiritual concerns of this period, include the following three authors. Not all of the entries for each author or composer are listed. The full citations are provided to demonstrate the maturity of musical awareness and expertise which the Brethren of that era had possessed.

Ora W. Garber (1903–1981) authored Hymn 275, *"'Tis Not With Eyes of Flesh We See"* [HWB 571]. His text was set to the tune ST. PETERSBURG by D. S. Bortniansky (1752–1825). Stanza one reads:

> *'Tis not with eyes of flesh we see*
> *That Christ is God's anointed one.*
> *With eyes of faith we know that he*
> *Is God's beloved only Son –*
> *Eternal King enthroned above,*
> *Revealer of God's grace and love.*

Kenneth I. Morse (1913–1999) offered an altered version of *"Is There a God?"* (Hymn 77, Author Unknown), drawn from *The Brethren's Tune and Hymn Book* (1872). As mentioned above, the tune PIONEER by Nevin W. Fisher, to which the hymn text was wedded, was a revision of the tune ASHLAND by J. C. Ewing included in *The Brethren Hymnody With Tunes* (1884).

If there is one hymn for which Morse is especially remembered, it is Hymn 225, "Move in Our Midst" [HWB 418]. The tune, PINE GLEN, was composed by Perry L. Huffaker (1902–1982). All stanzas are given here.

> *Move in our midst, thou Spirit of God;*
> *Go with us down from thy holy hill;--.*
> *Walk with us through the storm and the calm;*
> *Spirit of God, go thou with us still.*
>
> *Touch thou our hands to lead us aright;*
> *Guide us forever, show us thy way.*
> *Transform our darkness into thy light;*
> *Spirit of God, lead thou us today.*

Strike from our feet the fetters that bind;
Lift from our lives the weight of our wrong.
Teach us to love with heart, soul, and mind;
Spirit of God, thy love makes us strong.

Kindle our hearts to burn with thy flame;
Raise up thy banners high in this hour.
Stir us to build new worlds in thy name;
Spirit of God, O send us thy pow'r!

Albert Cassel Wieand's hymn, "On the Radiant Threshold" (Hymn 65), discussed in the survey of *The Brethren Hymnal* (1901), is included again here and in *Hymnal: A Worship Book* (1992) as Hymn 649. It was set to the tune BE THOU OUR GUIDE by George B. Holsinger. There are also twenty-three metricizations of Psalms included in *The Brethren Hymnal* (1951), such as *"How Lovely is Thy Dwelling Place"* (Hymn 3, for Psalm 84) by Alvin Frantz Brightbill.

In addition, Brethren tune composers are well represented. Some composers listed with the Brethren authors above may be repeated here because of the tune names which have interest to Brethren. Not all Brethren included in the hymnal are given here:

> William Beery (1852–1956): 88, 298 [HUNTINGDON], 323 [ELGIN], 361[JOHN NAAS], 454 [JUNIATA]
> Alvin Franz Brightbill (1903–1976): 3, 330, 392, 412, 415, 492, 517, 588, 677
> Ernestine Hoff Emrick (b. 1918): 30
> J. C. Ewing (1849–1937): 77 & 609 [ASHLAND, arr. by Nevin Fisher and renamed PIONEER]
> Nevin W. Fisher (1900–1984): 34, 77 [PIONEER], 111, 127, 137, 202, 212, 304 [BRIDGEWATER], 307, 365, 385 [MCPHERSON], 386 [HIGHLAND AVENUE], 411, 476, 493, 498, 499, 609 [PIONEER]

Donald Frederick (b. 1917): 110 [JAMES QUINTER], 173, 223, 486, 487, 488, 489, 606 [MACK], 654

Henry G. Gottshall (1903–1946): 418 [CHRISTOPHER SOWER]

Edyth Hillery Hay (1891–1943): 456 [HILLERY]

George B. Holsinger (1857–1908): 65, 265 [HOLSINGER], 410

Perry L. Huffaker (1902–1982): 72, 86, 225, 265 [Arr. G. B. Holsinger's Tune HOLSINGER], 281, 370, 372, 439, 467

Nelson T. Huffman (1901–1992): 655, 658

Kenneth I. Morse (1913–1999): 370

Florence Ziegler Sanger (b. 1906): 509

J. Henry Showalter (1864–1947): 162, 218 [SHOWALTER], 291, 430, 456, 458, 497, 599 [MOHLER].

Significant non-Brethren tune composers and sources given below indicate the selection of tunes was not made merely by their popularity, but rather by well-educated musicians who knew music history, and who were striving to include in some cases tunes which reflected the Brethren German roots.

Johann Sebastian Bach (1685–1750)
Bohemian Brethren Gesangbuch (1566)
Freylinghausen's *Gesangbuch* (1704)
Geistliche Kirchengesang (1623)
Klug's *Gesangbuch* (1535)
Lüneburgisches Gesangbuch (1686)
Martin Luther (1483–1546)
Lyra Davidica (1708)
Meiningisches Gesangbuch (1693)
Musikalisches Handbuch, Hamburg (1690)
Praxis Pietatis Melica, Crüger (1653, 1688)
Wittenberg Gesangbuch (1535).

Other significant non-Brethren authors represented include: James Montgomery (1771–1854), 9 hymns; Isaac Watts (1674–1748), 17 hymns; Charles Wesley (1707–1788), 12 hymns; George Whitefield (1714–1770), 1 hymn; and John Greenleaf Whittier (1807–1892), 6 hymns.

Another distinctive feature of *The Brethren Hymnal* (1951) is a section of fifty-seven gospel songs, referred to as 'Songs of Salvation'. There was reluctance on the part of the hymnal committee to include these because, in their view: "They distract from genuine worship and are psychologically disintegrating in their efforts upon groups and individuals."[171]

A section on "Worship Aids" included some entries to be sung by choir alone or with congregation, and those to be spoken either by the pastoral leadership or with the congregation. The sung aids include Invocations, Calls to Worship, Ascriptions of Praise, Antiphons, Calls to Prayer, Responses After Prayer, Responses to Scripture, Offertory Sentences, Benedictions, and Amen's. Spoken aids include Responsive Readings, Unison Readings, Calls to Worship, Invocations, Prayers of Confession, Assurances of Pardon, Offertory Sentences, Offertory Prayers, and Benedictions. All these were included to assist pastors and congregations to worship in ways the hymnal committee believed was appropriate liturgically.

A summary description of the hymnal was given by Donald Durnbaugh:

> The large selection of hymns and worship resources in the present *Brethren Hymnal* indicates the ecumenical nature of contemporary Brethren worship, for the present hymnal is replete with social-gospel hymns, classical hymns of Protestantism, gospel songs from

---

[171] Ibid., 521.

> revivalism, and older and newer selections from Brethren authors and composers.[172]

The compilation of *The Brethren Hymnal* (1951) reflects careful scholarship in the listing of sources, adaptations and alterations of hymns, and the inclusion of meter designations which were absent in *Hymnal: Church of the Brethren* (1925). The 1951 hymnal may most certainly be included in a remark by distinguished musicologist Robert Stevenson (1916–2012) in his survey of *Protestant Church Music in America*: "The hymnals of the larger denominations grow more and more 'respectable' musically with each new edition."[173]

Anniversary Hymns (1958)

One additional publication in this Evolving era was *Anniversary Hymns*,[174] a small pamphlet produced for the 250th anniversary of the Brethren in 1958. Included was Alexander Mack's hymn *"Count the Cost,"* at that time recently discovered. The text was translated by Ora W. Garber, and wedded to a chorale tune by Johann Hermann Schein (1586–1630), harmonized by Johann Sebastian Bach (1785–1750). Also presented was *"God of the Nations"* by Edward K. Ziegler (1903–1989) set with Ernestine Hoff Emrick's tune ANNIVERSARY.

End of an Era

With respect to the changes over time and the resultant fabric of Brethren hymnody by mid-twentieth century, Hedda Durnbaugh offered the following conclusions:

---

[172] Donald F. Durnbaugh, *The Church of the Brethren Past and Present* (Elgin, IL: The Brethren Press, 1971), 65.

[173] Robert Stevenson, *Protestant Church Music in America* (New York: W. W. Norton, 1966), 126.

[174] *Anniversary Hymns,* (Elgin, IL: Church of the Brethren General Offices, 1958).

> In surveying the route which Brethren hymnody has taken, one observes not an adaptation but rather an acculturation to the Anglo-American situation. Heritage and piety of the German hymnody faded away as English language and English hymnody increased in importance and influence. The few translations of German hymns that were received into the English hymnals of the Brethren did not enter in a direct line from their German ones but were probably selected from other contemporary hymnbooks, a customary way of hymnal compiling. The small percentage of German hymns in English translation does not constitute a recovery and consciousness of the German hymnic heritage of the Brethren. Thus, in the area of hymnody, the Brethren have lost their German heritage, and along with it, the type of piety and spirituality that the hymns reflect ... Brethren hymnody increasingly took on the features of British Victorian and American nineteenth-century conventional hymnody, with an infusion of original but rather mainline-oriented hymnody towards the middle of the twentieth century. The acculturation is complete.[175]

Durnbaugh's remarks are incisive and well-received, especially because of her passion for the German heritage and hymnody. Her great gift to the Brethren, including this writer, has been her superior hymnological work, *The German Hymnody of the Brethren 1720–1903*, cited frequently in this study. We appreciate and understand her lament over the lack of more German heritage hymns in Brethren hymnals of the twentieth century. Little attention to the heritage hymns was paid in the 1925 hymnal. However, the heritage is represented in the 1951 hymnal at least through the translations of a number of German hymns. They may not have entered the hymnal in a direct line

---

[175] H. T. Durnbaugh, "Changes Reflected in Brethren Hymnody," 200–202.

from their German counterparts; nevertheless, they entered, and they did so by those who may not have been attempting to recover the German hymnody heritage, but rather simply and intentionally to include a sampling of the heritage for contemporary Brethren Christians to appreciate. *The Brethren Hymnal* (1951) was a very successful venture. It represented significant maturation and evolution of Brethren spiritual thought and practice.

Endeavoring: Later 20th Century to 2008

There remains one more era of Brethren hymnody. It is the period from the last third of the twentieth century through 2008. The heading "Endeavoring" is used to refer to the on-going attempt, even struggle, to try to cope with and relate to the cultural changes in society and express the relevancy of the church, its message and mission for contemporary culture. Whereas the 1951 hymnal was, among other things, an expression of the committee's desire to advance the more formal corporate worship elements and ordering similar with other mainline Protestant churches, and to demonstrate scholarly respectability, hymnic activity in the second half of the century endeavored to find ways to express the church's relevance to society amidst significant membership decline.

The Brethren Songbook (1974, 1979)

The Brethren Songbook (1974) and *The Brethren Songbook* (1979) were produced with such a goal in mind. Conceived in part as supplements to *The Brethren Hymnal* (1951), they contained more contemporary hymnic expressions, some with guitar chords marked and piano accompaniment provided. Kenneth I. Morse's text, *"Brothers and Sisters of Mine,"* set to the tune MINE ARE THE HUNGRY by Wilbur E. Brumbaugh (1931–1977) in *The Brethren Songbook* (1974) [also HWB 142], is a superior hymn in every way: as literature, as message, as music, and as an example of what spiritual themes were important to Brethren at this time. The four stanzas of this hymn of Christian responsibility and social concern are given here:

> *Brothers and sisters of mine are the hungry,*
> *Who sigh in their sorrow and weep in their pain.*
> *Sisters and brothers of mine are the homeless,*
> *Who wait without shelter from wind and from rain.*

> *Strangers and neighbors, they claim my attention.*
> *They sleep by my door-step, they sit by my bed.*
> *Neighbors and strangers, their anguish concerns me,*
> *And I must not feast till the hungry are fed.*
>
> *People are they, men and women and children,*
> *And each has a heart keeping time with my own.*
> *People are they, persons made in God's image,*
> *So what shall I offer them, bread or a stone?*
>
> *Lord of all living, we make our confession:*
> *Too long we have wasted the wealth of our lands.*
> *Lord of all loving, renew our compassion,*
> *And open our hearts while we reach out our hands.*

Most likely sensing uncertain days in the direction of worship and music, and desiring to educate the next generation of the Brethren, Kenneth I. Morse, Church of the Brethren elder, journalist, editor, poet and song writer, authored a modest-sized study book on worship for pastors and parishioners. The book's title, *Move in Our Midst*, was the same as Morse's well-known and loved hymn (225) in *The Brethren Hymnal* (1951).

Developments

In addition, the Church of the Brethren, as well as The Brethren Church and the Grace Brethren churches, had to wrestle with the significant and controversial influences and developments within society and the Church. The emergence of the "Praise and Worship" genre of congregational song, a direct outgrowth of the Charismatic Movement, contributed to the confusion and strain of just how to do music in the church, especially by those representing the Evolving era of liturgical education, hymn writing and composing, and hymnal compilation. The advent of the "Praise Team" with drum set and microphones held by team members, often leading the congregation initially in singing songs of a more "ballad" nature than those of stanzaic, syllabic accessibility, served to polarize congregations. For many, worship was coming apart at the proverbial seams. The new music was viewed by most of the scholarly church musicians as a "dumbing down" of literary, theological, and musical quality.

Added to the above has been the influence of the feminist movement and discussions over sexual orientation. As a result, the use of inclusive language in hymn writing and singing, and of altering texts was encouraged in mainline hymnody.

Along with all of this is the lack of ability by so many newer parishioners to sing in parts (harmony), probably in part due to the influences of popular music and music technology, and music education practices in public schools. Interestingly, singing in unison (melody only), is not unlike the early Brethren practice. Have we come full circle? Is this a period of restart, a new emergence of the church? It has seemed so.

So how would a committee, if there would be a need for one, address or not address the above and any other worship and social concerns in the selection of the congregational song literature for the compilation of a new hymnal?

Hymnal: A Worship Book (1992) and Hymnal Companion (1996); Hymnal Supplement (2001 & Periodically Onward)

While it may be correct to say *The Brethren Hymnal* (1951) reflected an ecumenical musical diet in Brethren worship at that time, the most recent Brethren hymnal, *Hymnal: A Worship Book* (1992), is not only ecumenical and eclectic in its contents, but also in production, due in part most likely to financial concerns. The 1992 hymnal was published jointly by the Church of the Brethren, the General Conference Mennonite Church, and the Mennonite Church in North America. Nancy Rosenberger Faus, Professor at Bethany Theological Seminary and Chair of the hymnal committee, described the significance of the contents:

> By the time of publication, 658 hymns and responses and over 200 worship resources, including scripture readings had been selected for inclusion. Over 200 texts from the 1951 hymnal also were included. More than 100 texts, tunes, or translations are by Brethren and Mennonite writers and composers. The hymnal encompasses all musical eras and styles, from chants to chorales to contemporary texts and tunes, including African-American spirituals and black gospel, Taizé "sung prayers," gospel songs, and songs from Asia, Hispanic, Native American and African sources (most including their native language). Over 80 chorale-like selections represent the German roots of the participating denominations. Two hundred hymns and songs were written since the mid-1960s influenced by inclusive language concerns.[176]

Unlike *Hymnal: Church of the Brethren* (1925) which contained no hymns on feet-washing, *Hymnal: A Worship Book* (1992) was produced with "eagerness to sustain denominational and historical tradition ..."[177] For example, the "servant" theme is present in Hymn 307, *"Will You Let Me Be Your Servant."* Feetwashing is implied in Hymn 450, *"Here in our Upper Room"* by Paul M. Robinson. However, for purposes of inclusive language, this was a 1990 revision of his hymn which first appeared as Hymn 508 in *The Brethren Hymnal* (1951). Stanza three is given here as it reads in The *Brethren Hymnal* (1951) followed by *Hymnal: A Worship Book* (1992).

---

[176] Nancy Rosenberger Faus, "Hymnal: A Worship Book," *The Brethren Encyclopedia,* Vol. 4, 2205.

[177] Ibid., 2206.

> *We share with Thee the feast of love*
> *As hearts are knit in brotherhood;*
> *O may Thy Spirit in us move*
> *Our wills to serve our brother's good.*

> *We share with you the feast of love*
> *As hearts are knit in one accord.*
> *Oh, may your Spirit in us move*
> *Our wills to love you more, dear Lord.*

Sometimes inclusive language can carry the author's original intent. Other times, as in this example, the alteration does not preserve it. In an attempt to be sensitive to matters of inclusion, the appropriateness of altering another's work of art comes into question, unless of course the changes were made by the original author.

Additional notable features of the 1992 hymn book are two categories of "Heritage Hymns." Among the "Heritage Hymns: Anabaptist (16th–18th c.)" is Hymn 407, *"We are People of God's Peace,"* by Menno Simons (1496–1561), translated by Esther C. Bergen (b. 1921). Stanza three reads:

> *We are servants of God's peace,*
> *Of the new creation.*
> *Choosing peace, we faithfully*
> *Serve with heart's devotion.*
> *Jesus Christ, the Prince of Peace,*
> *Confidence will give us.*
> *Christ the Lord is our defense;*
> *Christ will never leave us.*[178]

---

[178] Menno Simons, 1552; tr. Esther Bergen, Mennonite World Conference Songbook, 1990 Translation copyright © 1990; Mennonite World Conference.

Also in this category is Hymn 438, *"I sing with exultation"* by Felix Mantz (c.1498–1527), translated by Marion Wenger (b. 1932) and altered by Harris J. Loewen (b. 1953). Stanza four of this hymn for baptism says:

> *Christ bid us, none compelling,*
> *To his glorious throne.*
> *They only who are willing*
> *Christ as Lord to own,*
> *They are as assured of heaven,*
> *Who will right faith pursue,*
> *With hearts made pure do penance,*
> *Sealed in baptism true.*

"The Heritage Hymns: Brethren (18th c.)" include four hymns we have reviewed previously: Hymn 437, *"Count Well the Cost"* by Alexander Mack Sr; Hymn 40, *"Jesus Christ, God's Only Son"* by Alexander Mack Jr; Hymn 549, *"Savior of My Soul"* by Johannes Naas; and Hymn 451, Wilhelm Knepper's *"How Pleasant is It."*[179]

Other Brethren authors and composers include many familiar and some new names. Some of the authors and composers appearing in Brethren hymnals for the first time include Anne Metzler Albright (b. 1925), author of Hymn 378, *"By Peter's House."* Stanza one and the refrain read:

---

[179] One correction should be made regarding the source information for *"How Pleasant Is It."* The HWB says the source of Knepper's hymn is drawn from 'Freylinghausen's *Geistreiches Gesangbuch* 1720', which is not the case, because the Freylinghausen hymn book with the same name was published at Halle in two installments, 1704 and 1714, before Knepper authored his hymn text from the prison at Solingen. Rather, Knepper's hymn is from the first Brethren hymnbook, *Geistreiches Gesangbuch* 1720 published by Christopher Konert at Berleberg.

> *By Peter's house in village fair,*
> *You met the sick and healed them there.*
> *Down crowded path the woman trod*
> *To touch the robe of the Son of God.*

Refrain

> *O Jesus of the healing hem and*
> *Hand and heart, heal us as them!*

Wilbur E. Brumbaugh, in addition to composing MINE ARE THE HUNGRY for Kenneth I. Morse's *"Brothers and Sisters of Mine"* cited above, composed O GOD OF MYSTERY for Morse's *"O God of Mystery and Might"* (Hymn 130). This is another winning combination. Stanza one reads:

> *O God of mystery and might,*
> *Great Mover of the stars in flight,*
> *Alert our hearts to apprehend*
> *The silent witnesses you send.*

Joan Fyock Norris (b. 1938), certainly one of the finer church musicians, composers and arrangers of this era, composed the tune McRAE for Hymn 200, *"Where is this Stupendous Stranger?"* The quality text is by poet Christopher Smart (1722–1771). All four stanzas are presented here.

> *Where is this stupendous Stranger?*
> *Prophets, shepherds, kings, advise!*
> *Lead me to the Master's manger,*
> *Show me where my Savior lies.*
>
> *O most Mighty, O most Holy,*
> *Far beyond the seraph's thought,*
> *Art thou then so mean and lowly*
> *As unheeded prophets thought?*

> *Oh, the magnitude of meekness!*
> *Worth from worth immortal sprung!*
> *Oh, the strength of infant weakness,*
> *If eternal is so young!*
>
> *God all bounteous, all creative,*
> *Whom no ills from good dissuade,*
> *Is incarnate and a native*
> *Of the very world he made.*

Fyock Norris was also writer and compiler of the very fine *Hymnal Companion* (1996) to *Hymnal: A Worship Book*, giving notes on the hymns, authors of hymns and worship aids, translators, and composers.[180]

Kenneth I. Morse, who wrote "Strangers No More" (Hymn 322), teamed up with composer Dianne Huffman Morningstar (b. 1944), who provided the tune STRANGERS NO MORE. Their winning combination captured some of the sentiments of contemporary Christian concern. The hymn begins with the Refrain.

> *For we are strangers no more, but members of one family,*
> *Strangers no more, but part of one humanity;*
> *Strangers no more, we're neighbors to each other now;*
> *Strangers no more, we're sisters and we're brothers now.*

Stanza two says:

> *Where diff'ring cultures meet we'll serve together.*
> *Where hatred rages we will strive for peace.*

---

[180] Joan A. Fyock, Writer/Compiler, Lani Wright, Editor, *Hymnal Companion: Prepared by Churches in the Believers Church Tradition* (Elgin, IL: Brethren Press; Newton, KS: Faith and Life Press; Scottdale, PA: Mennonite Publishing House, 1996).

> *Come, take my hand, and we will pray together*
> *That justice come and strife and warfare cease.*

Kenneth L. Gibble (b. 1941) authored "Spirit, Blowing and Blazing," and composed the tune for it, BLAZING SPIRIT, included as Hymn 1012 in the *Hymnal Supplement* (Elgin, IL: Brethren Press, 2001 and periodically onward). Stanza one of Gibble's excellent text reads:

> *Spirit, blowing and blazing,*
> *Pentecost wind and Pentecost flame,*
> *Spirit of power, invade this hour.*
> *Blow, Spirit, burn, as when you first came.*

Gibble also authored Hymn 1102, "God of Creation." Stanza one reads:

> *God of creation, show us your glory,*
> *Splendored in sunshine, shadowed in night,*
> *Maker and Shaper, tell us the Story,*
> *Of your great mercy, justice and might.*

The tune for this hymn was composed by Richard D. Brode (b. 1963). This tune and others by Brode (e.g. NEW BEGINNINGS, for Brian Wren's *"This is a Day of New Beginnings,"* Hymn 640 in *Hymnal: A Worship Book*) are noteworthy.

As mentioned previously, it is with sincere apology that we are unable to mention all of the many fine authors and composers of the Endeavoring era in the Church of the Brethren. The intention here has been not to present a comprehensive overview of Brethren hymnody; but rather to discuss the spiritual themes of the Brethren expressed in examples of their hymnody through the rich and most interesting history of the first 300 years of the Brethren movement. William Beery's *Brethren Hymns, Hymnals, Authors and Composers: A Study in*

Our Literary and Musical Heritage (1945), *Handbook on Brethren Hymns* (1959) by Ruth B. Statler (1906–2008) and Nevin W. Fisher, and *Hymnal Companion* (1996) compiled by Joan Fyock Norris, provide biographical material on other Brethren authors and composers.

German Baptist Brethren Youth Sing

A special development within the Old German Baptist Brethren is worth noting. On April 6, 2001, this writer attended a "Youngfolks Sing and Learn" event, held at the 4-H Building in Flora, Indiana. The youth of the church had been practicing music to present publicly, in their view not as a concert, but rather as a "Sing & Learn" experience. The learning included being able to *sing in parts*. The young folks were "coached" by two couples and a single woman. Boys and girls sang together as "Mixed Voices," singing "Drills," and hymns such as "Lo How a Rose," "Praise Him! Praise Him," "Seek Ye First," "You Are My All in All," "Great is Thy Faithfulness," and "The Lord Bless You and Keep You." The girls sang a few pieces, such as "Come to the Water," "The Rose," and "Love Will Bring Us Together." Also, the boys sang alone: "Rise Up Ye Men of God," "The King is Coming," and "Were You There." The singing was still unaccompanied, yet it was, in this writer's view, a wonderful, and shall we say progressive development that youth of one of the most conservative Brethren varieties are learning to sing in harmony.

End of Another Era

To close this era, I shall mention my own tune, DEVOTION, set to a hymnic version of The Lord's Prayer, "Our Father in Heaven," by Sarah J. Hale (1788–1879). This text is included as Hymn 108 in the Old Order German Baptist Brethren hymnbook, *A Collection of Hymns and Sacred Songs* (1882 onward). Hale, a native of Newport, New Hampshire, was a novelist, and editor of *Godey's Lady's Book*, the best known women's periodical of its day. She was the author of the well-known children's poem, "Mary Had a Little Lamb," and was instrumental in persuading President Abraham Lincoln to support legislation establishing a national holiday of Thanksgiving in 1863. The two stanzas of her hymn text read:

> *Our Father in heaven,*
> *We hallow Thy name;*
> *May Thy kingdom holy*
> *On earth be the same;*
> *Oh, give to us daily*
> *Our portion of bread;*
> *It is from Thy bounty*
> *That all must be fed.*
>
> *Forgive our transgressions,*
> *And teach us to know*
> *That humble compassion*
> *Which pardons each foe;*
> *Keep us from temptation,*
> *From evil and sin,*
> *And thine be the glory*
> *Forever. Amen!*

In addition, what follows is the text of Alexander Mack's *"Count Well the Cost"* as adapted by this writer, set with the tune HENDON and sung at the 300th Anniversary Conference of the Brethren in Richmond, Virginia in 2008.[181]

---

[181] Original Text by Alexander Mack Sr. (1679–1735), Source: *Geistreiches Gesang-Buch*, 1720, translated by Ora W. Garber (1903–1981), Copyright 1958 by the General Brotherhood of the Church of the Brethren, as given in *The Complete Writings of Alexander Mack*, William R. Eberly, Editor, Winona Lake,

JESUS says "Count Well the Cost"
When the pledge of faith you make.
Are you sure though all seem lost,
All you'll risk for His dear sake,
All you'll risk for His dear sake?

In CHRIST'S death you're buried now,
Union through this sacred sign;
Self no claim you dare allow,
Fellowship is your design,
Fellowship is your design.

In the Church's sheltering fold
Molded is the child of GOD.
Learning as the Word is told,
Saved we are by JESUS' blood,
Saved we are by JESUS' blood.

Let us serve, the time is right,
His the will to reach the lost.
CHRIST Himself joins in the fight,
He who counted well the cost,
He who counted well the cost.[182]

IN: BMH Books, 1991, 107–109.

Adaptation by Peter E. Roussakis (b. 1946); Tune: HENDON 7.7.7.7.7. by Henri A. Cesar Malan (1787–1864); Adaptation & Setting © 2005 Peter E. Roussakis.

[182] The scores for both the tune DEVOTION and the setting of "Count Well the Cost" are available by request from the author. Books by Peter E. Roussakis include those published by Meetinghouse Press: *Classic Worship: With Brethren in Mind; United in Prayer: Understanding and Praying the Lord's Prayer;* and the above mentioned *John Cook Ewing (1849–1937): Pioneer Brethren Musician, Teacher and Composer* (with William Beery).

Postscript

Brethren have always been a singing people. Whether they sang unaccompanied or with instruments, in unison or with harmony, in German or in English, using hymnbooks without or with musical notation, Brethren have sung God's greatness and goodness, majesty and mercy. They have proclaimed God who is powerful, and they have surrendered themselves to God's personal will and ways. Through their hymns they have prayed, pleaded with the lost, reflected upon their pilgrimage, expressed reliance upon God through the struggles, and sung in anticipation of our eternal home with Christ.

Brethren have been cautious about the way they sang, and they have let it loose! Hymn writing, composing and singing have been outward vehicles expressing inner devotion. Brethren have called one another to deny the world, and they have embraced good aspects of it. They have resisted change, and they have adapted to changes in communication.

They have taught through hymns and hymn singing, called one another to pious living, and held firmly to the truths of scripture in thought and practice. Brethren have been absorbed with death and dying in hymns, and they have sung with joyful anticipation of the victory to come.

Brethren have focused on doctrine in hymns, and they have sung with evangelistic fervor. They have been plain in worship, become more formal in worship, and tried to relate to contemporary society through informal practices of worshiping and singing.

Inner devotional matters and outward social concerns have been expressed in their hymnody. Whether liberal, moderate or conservative, Brethren have and continue to be a singing people, expressing their "*Piety in Song*".

Index (With Selected Hymn Texts, Tunes, Authors and Composers)

A Choice Selection of Hymns (1830), 57
A Collection of Hymns and Sacred Songs (1882), 78-80, 87, 134-135
A Collection of Hymns for Sunday Schools and Public and Private Devotion (1879), 88
A Collection of Psalms, Hymns, and Spiritual Songs (1867), 12, 13 (note), 66, 68-72, 74, 83, 88
A Selection of Hymns (1816), 51, 57
A soul which loves God (A. Mack Jr.; trans., S. Heckman), 33
Acculturation, 108, 123
Ach wie solieblich und wie fein (*How Pleasant is It*, W. Knepper; trans., O. Garber), 26, 130 (& note)
Albright, Anne Metzler (b. 1925), 130-131
ALLE MENSCHEN MÜSSEN STERBEN (J. S. Bach), 46
Almighty Sov'reign of the Skies, 83
Anglo-American, 93, 123
ANNIVERSARY (E. H. Emrick), 122
Anniversary Hymns (1958), 122
Anointing, 63, 79
Arnold, Gottfried (1666-1714), 14-15, 23, 29
ASHLAND (J. C. Ewing), 83, 118-119
Ashland College, 66, 82
Awake, Ye Young Heroes (*Ihr jungen Helden aufgewacht*, W. Knepper; trans., H. Durnbaugh), 27, 56, 58
Bach, Johann Sebastian (1685-1750), 46, 117, 120, 122
Bailey, Albert Edward (1871-1951), 105 (& note)
Bamberger, Christian (1801-1880), 60, 73
Baptism, 23, 28, 36, 55, 63, 67
BAPTISMAL HYMN (J. C. Ewing), 85
Barnby, Sir Joseph (1838-1896), 113
Barth, Karl (1886-1968), 13
BE THOU OUR GUIDE (G. B. Holsinger), 119

Becker, Peter (1687–1758), 27–29, 36–37, 71, 73
Beery, Adaline (1859–1929), 89, 96–97, 102
Beery, William (1852–1956), 43, 78 (& note), 87–89, 92, 97, 101–102, 112, 119, 133–134
Beethoven, Ludwig van (1770–1837), 114
Befiehl du deine Wenge (*Give to the Winds Your Fears*, P. Gerhardt; trans., J. Wesley), 22, 107, 114
Beissel, Johann Conrad (1691–1768), 36 (note)
Benson, Louis F. (1855–1930), 50, 82, 108
Bergen, Esther C. (b. 1921), 129
Bethany Theological Seminary, 96, 116, 127
Bible School Echoes, and Sacred Hymns (1880), 82 (note)
BLAZING SPIRIT (K. Gibble), 133
Bliss, Philip (1833–1876), 97, 113
Blume, Friedrich (1893–1975), 22
Bourgeois, Louis (1500–1565), 114
Bowman, Carl F. (b. 1957), 61, 63, 68
Bradbury, William (1816–1868), 97, 113
Brethren Hymns, Hymnals, Authors and Composers, 133
BRIDGEWATER (N. Fisher), 119
Bridgewater College (Virginia Normal School), 83, 91
Brightbill, Alvin Franz (1903–1976), 116, 119
Broad spectrum of inclusions, 108
Brode, Richard D. (b. 1963), 133
Brotherhood and world peace, 109–111, 115
Brothers and Sisters of Mine (K. Morse), 125–126
Brumbaugh, H. B. (1836–1919), 75, 92
Brumbaugh, J. B. (1848–1922), 75
Brumbaugh, Wilbur E. (1931–1977), 125, 131
Bryant, William Cullen (1794–1878), 93, 108
By Peter's House (A. M. Albright), 130–131
Camp-meeting spirituals (bush-meeting songs), 48, 55, 58–59
Cassel, Abraham H. (1820–1908), 31
Cassel, Jacob C. (1849–1919), 100
Chief metaphor for Brethren spirituality, 3, 18–19, 43, 104

Choirs, 101, 116
Christen müssen sich hier schicken (*Christians here must suit themselves*, C. Sauer Jr.), 39–40
CHRISTOPHER SOWER (H. G. Gottshall), 120
Churchly hymns, 39, 53, 96
Click, Daniel Medford (1858–1947), 97
Conventicles, 25
COOK (W. Beery), 78
Count the Cost, Count Well the Cost (A. Mack Sr.), 23, 24 (& note), 28, 122, 130, 135–136 (& notes)
Cowper, William (1731–1800), 52, 70, 83, 93, 108
Croft, William (1678–1727), 114
Crosby, Fanny (1823–1915), 84, 93, 104, 108
Crüger, Johann (1598–1662), 21 (note), 22–23
Danner, Heinrich (1742–1814), 55, 60, 71, 73
Danner, Jakob (1727–c.1800), 37–38, 54–55, 71, 73
Das Christliche Gesang-Buch (1874), 72
Das Kleine Davidische Psalterspiel der Kinder Zions (1744), 29–32, 34, 36, 49, 54, 57, 74, 107
Davidische Psalter-Spiel der Kinder Zions (Inspirationist, 1718), 20, 21 (note), 29
Decius, Nikolaus (c.1490–1541), 117
Denial or self and the world, 74
DEVOTION (P. Roussakis), 134
Die Kleine Harfe (1792), 36–43, 49, 54
Die Kleine Lieder Sammlung (1826), 54–57
Die Kleine Perlen-Sammlung (1858), 57–60
Die sen Täufling wir (*We bring this person who wishes to be baptized*), 55
Doane, William, Howard (1832–1915), 113
Doddridge, Philip (1702–1751), 70, 93
Dunkard Brethren, 6, 87 (& note), 115
Dunker liturgy, 63
Durnbaugh, Donald F. (1927–2005), 99, 121–122, notes throughout

Durnbaugh, Hedwig T. (b. 1928), 3, 23, 27, 31, 49–50, 52, 55–56, 58–60, 66, 68, 75, 77–78, 93–94, 122–123, notes throughout
Dykes, John B. (1823–1876), 114
Eby, David F. (1828–1917), 81 (note)
Ecumenical, 99, 121, 127
EIN' FESTE BURG (M. Luther), 114
Ein Geistliches Magazein, 33
Ein Sammlung von Psalmen, Lobesängen, und Geistlichen Liedern (1893), 72
Eins betrübt mich sehr auf Erden (*I have felt great agitation*, Naas; trans., O. Garber), 41
ELGIN (W. Beery), 89, 119
ELGIN (G. B. Holsinger), 95, 97
Ellis, Charles Calvert (1874–1950), 100
Emrick, Ernestine Hoff (b. 1918), 119, 122
Eucharist (Communion), 28
Ewing, John Cook (1849–1937), 64, 66, 74–75, 76 (& note), 77, 78 (& note), 81–87, 89, 118–119
Faus, Nancy Rosenberger (b. 1934), 127
Fawcett, John (1740–1817), 93
Feetwashing, 26, 28, 79, 95–97, 128
Fisher, Nevin W. (1900–1984), 83, 101, 116, 118–119, 134
Flory, Gertrude A. (1862–1930), 89–90, 96, 102, 112
Flory, John S. (1866–1961), 19, 37, 50, 101
Following Jesus, Our Mighty Exemplar (C. L. Shacklock), 85
Formal worship, 102, 116, 121, 125
Franck, Johann (1618–1677), 21 (note), 22
Francke, August Hermann (1663–1727), 19
Frantz, Evelyn M. B., 114–115
Frantz, Michael (1687–1748), 16, 47
Fraternity of German Baptists, 6, 48, 68 (note)
Frederick, Donald (b. 1917), 120
Freylinghausen, Johann Anastasius (1670–1739), 19, 21 (note), 120

Friends, Good Night (*Gute Nacht, ihr meine Lieben*, J. Danner), 37–38, 54
Funk, Benjamin (1829–1909), 75
Fyock Norris, Joan A. (b. 1938), 131–132, 134
Gabriel, Charles H. (1856–1932), 113
Garber, Ora W. (1903–1981), 24, 26, 38, 41–42, 44–46, 55, 118, 122, 135 (note)
Garrett, Marguerite Bixler (1871–1963), 102, 112
Geh, Seele, Frisch in Glauben fort (*Go Forth, My Soul, Renewed in Faith*; trans. H. Durnbaugh), 56
Geistliches Gewürz-Gärtlein Heilsuchender Seelen (Spiritual Spice-Garden for Seeking Souls), 43–44
Geistreiches Gesang-Buch (Brethren, 1720), 19, 20 (& notes), 21–27, 29
Geistreiches Gesang-Buch (Freylinghausen, 1704, 1714), 19, 120
Gerhardt, Paul (1607–1676), 21 (note), 22, 29, 107–108, 114, 117
Gerlach, David (c.1811–1879), 60, 73
German chorale heritage, 11, 20–21 (& notes), 29, 117, 122
German (Brethren) hymn writers, 60, 73, 116–117
Germantown, 27–29
Gibble, Kenneth L. (b. 1941), 133
Give to the Winds Your Fears (*Befiehl du deine Wenge*, P. Gerhardt; trans., J. Wesley), 22, 107, 114
Go Forth, My Soul, Renewed in Faith (*Geh, Seele, Frisch in Glauben fort*; trans. H. Durnbaugh), 56
God Himself is Present (*Gott is gegenwärtig*, G. Tersteegen), 21 (note), 22
God of Creation (K. Gibble), 133
God of the Nations (E. K. Ziegler), 122
Gospel Chimes for Sunday Schools and Religious Meetings (1889), 89
Gospel hymn/song genre, 77–78, 81–83, 87–89, 97, 99, 113, 121
Gospel Songs and Hymns, No. 1, For the Sunday School, Prayer Meeting, Social Meeting, General Song Service (1898), 91

Gott is gegenwärtig (*God Himself is Present*, G. Tersteegen), 21 (note), 22
Gottshall, Henry G. (1903–1946), 120
Goven, G. E. M., 89
Gracious King, Enthroned Above (J. W. Wayland), 102
Grahe, William (1693–1763), 25
Grebil, Samuel (1809–1881), 60, 73
Greet One Another With a Kiss (S. Kinsey), 79–80
Grisso, Lillian (1899–1974), 42–43
Gumre, Johann (d.1738), 28
Gute Nacht, ihr meine Lieben (*Friends, Good Night*, J. Danner), 37–38, 54
Hale, Sarah J. (1788–1879), 134–135
Hall, J. Lincoln (1866–1930), 87
Haller, Jakob (c.1777–1865), 60, 73
Handbook on Brethren Hymns (1959), 134
Handel, George Frederic (1685–1759), 114
Hart, Joseph (1712–1768), 51, 69
Hay, Edith Hillery (1891–1943), 102, 113, 120
Hark, Ten Thousand Harps and Voices (T. Kelly; trans. W. Preiss), 58
Haydn, Joseph (1737–1806), 114
Hear, O Hear Us, Heavenly Father (M. B. Garrett), 102, 112
Heiland meiner Seel (*Savior of My Soul*, J. Naas; trans., O Garber; paraphrased, L. Grisso), 42–43, 116, 130
Here in Our Upper Room with Thee (P. M. Robinson), 128–129
Heritage Hymns: Anabaptist, 129–130
Heritage Hymns: Brethren, 130
HIGHLAND AVENUE (N. Fisher), 119
Hiller, Philipp Friedrich (1699–1769), 72
HILLERY (E. H. Hay), 120
Hinks, Donald R., 57
Hochenau, Ernst Christoph Hochmann von (1670–1721), 23
Hoffer, J., 60, 73
Holmes, Oliver Wendell (1809–1894), 93, 108

HOLSINGER (G. B. Holsinger; arr. P. Huffaker), 120
Holsinger, George B. (1857–1908), 89, 91–92, 95, 97–98, 113, 119, 120
Holsinger, H. R. (1833–1905), 28, 75
Holsinger, L. T. (1850–1937), 92
Holsinger, Sallie Kagey, 96
Holy kiss, 63, 79–80, 115
Hoover, S. M., 94–95
How Lovely in Thy Dwelling Place (A. Brightbill), 119
How Pleasant is It (*Ach wie solieblich und wie fein*, W. Knepper; trans., O. Garber), 26, 130 (& note)
Huffaker, Perry L. (1902–1982), 118, 120
Huffman, Nelson T. (1901–1992), 120
HUNTINGDON (W. Beery), 89, 102, 112, 119
HUNTINGDON (J. C. Ewing), 84
Huntingdon Normal School (Juniata College), 66, 76, 89
Hymn festivals, 116
Hymn sings, 87
Hymnal: A Worship Book (1992), 39, 102, 127–133
Hymnal: Church of the Brethren (1925), 89, 101–115
Hymnal Companion (1996), 127, 132, 134
Hymnal Supplement (2001f.), 127, 133
Hymns for Closing, 102
Hymns for Opening, 101
Hymns for Worship and Songs of the Gospel (1909), 87
Hymns in German piety, 3, 23
Hymns of Awakening, 56, 72, 74
Hymns of "human-composure", 51
Hymns of Invitation, 56, 72, 74, 103
I have felt great Agitation (*Eins betrübt mich sehr auf Erden*, Naas; trans. O. Garber), 41
I sing with exhultation (F. Mantz), 130
I Will Not be Afraid (W. Beery), 89
If I Your Lord Have Washed Your Feet (J. W. Wayland), 95–96

Ihr jungen Helden aufgewacht (*Awake, Ye Young Heroes*, W. Knepper; trans., H. Durnbaugh), 27, 56, 58
In the Hour of Trial (J. Montgomery), 105–106
Inclusive language, 127–129
Ingalls, Jeremiah (1764–1828), 97
Ingredients in music, 12 (& note)
Inward, outward, 11, 14, 16, 34, 35 (note), 47–48, 53–54, 61, 63, 115
Is There a God? (anon.), 83
JAMES QUINTER (D. Frederick), 120
JESU MEINE FREUDE (J. Crüger), 21 (note), 22
Jesus Christ, God's Only Son (*Jesus Christus, Gottes Sohn*, A. Mack Jr.; trans., O. Garber), 38–39, 117, 130
Jesu meine Freude (*Jesus, Priceless Treasure*, J. Franck), 21 (note), 22
JOHN NAAS (W. Beery), 43, 119
JUNIATA (W. Beery), 102, 119
JUNIATA (J. C. Ewing), 84
Juniata College (Huntingdon Normal School), 66, 89
Kelly, Thomas (1769–1856), 58
Ken, Thomas (1637–1711), 52, 108
Kinsey, Samuel (1832–1883), 79–80
Kingdom Songs: For Sunday School, Prayer Meeting, Christian Workers' Societies, and All Seasons of Praise (1911), 91
Kingdom Songs, No. 2 (1918), 91
Kirkpatrick, William (1838–1921), 113
Knepper, Wilhelm (1691–c.1743), 25–27, 29, 56, 58, 71, 73, 130
Know Ye What I Have Done to You (J. W. Wayland), 95
Koch, Stephen (d. 1763), 27
Konert, Christopher, 19, 130 (note)
Krefeld, 27, 40
Kurtz, Henry (1796–1864), 54 (& note), 55 (note), 57, 70, 73
Langer, Suzanne K. (1895–1985), 11 (note)
Laying on of hands, 63
Lear, John W. (1870–1959), 113

Leibert, John, 51
Leibert, Peter (1727–1812), 33, 49
Liebe, Christian (1679–1757), 27
Lining hymns, 62 (note), 64, 88
Liturgical restraint, 63
Lo, a Gleam from Yonder Heaven (A. Beery), 102
LOBE DEN HERREN (*Stralsund Gesangbuch*, 1665; arr. in *Praxis Pietatis Melica*, 1688),
Lobe den Herren den mächitgen (*Praise to the Lord, the Almighty*, J. Neander), 21 (note), 22
Loewen, Harris J. (b. 1953), 130
Longenecker, Stephen L., 111, 115
Lord, With Devotion We Pray (E. H. Hay), 102, 113
Lord's Prayer, 62–63, 115, 134
Lorenz, Edmund S. (1854–1942), 97
Love feast, Lord's Supper, Communion, Eucharist, 28, 63 (& note),
Love Makes the Humble Service Sweet (J. W. Wayland), 95
LOWLY SERVICE (W. Beery), 97
Lowry, Robert (1829–1899), 97, 113
Luther, Martin (1483–1546), 11, 12 (& note), 13 (note), 20 (& note), 21, 114, 120
MACK (D. Frederick), 120
Mack Jr., Alexander (1712–1803), 19, 31–36, 38–39, 43, 71, 73, 84, 117
Mack Sr., Alexander (1679–1735), 6, 19, 23–25, 28–29, 37, 43, 73, 130, 135–136
Mainline-ism, 108, 116, 123, 127
Mantz, Felix (c. 1498–1527), 130
Marionborne, 25, 27, 40
Martin, Dennis D., 13–14, 18, 61, 100, 115
Mason, Lowell (1792–1872), 97, 114
MCPHERSON (N. Fisher), 119
MCRAE (J. Fyock Norris), 131
Meetinghouses, 46

Mein Jesu kaufte mich mit Blut (*My Jesus Purchased Me with Blood*, W. Preiss; trans., H. Durnbaugh), 58–59
Mendelssohn, Felix (1809–1847), 117
Merrill, William Pierson (1867–1954), 108–111
Metricizations of psalms, 119
Meyer Sr., Jakob W. (1832–1906), 60, 73
MEYERSDALE (J. C. Ewing), 84
Miles, C. Austin (1868–1946), 87
Miller, Abraham (d.1843), 60, 73
Miller, D. L. (1841–1921), 92
Miller, S. D., 60, 73
MINE ARE THE HUNGRY (W. Brumbaugh), 125
MOHLER (J. H. Showalter), 120
MONCE (J. C. Ewing), 84
Montgomery, James (1771–1854), 93, 104–106, 121
Morse, Kenneth I. (1913–1999), 83, 118, 120, 125–126, 131–133
Morningstar, Dianne Huffman (b. 1944), 132
Mother-hymns, 59
Move in Our Midst (book, K. Morse), 126
Move in Our Midst (hymn, K. Morse), 118–119, 126
Mozart, Wolfgang Amadeus (1756–1791), 114
Müller, Joseph (1707–1761), 36
Music as tonal analogue, 11 (note)
Music responses, 121, 128
Musical instruments, 36, 63–64, 67, 100–101, 115, 126
Musical notation, 64, 67, 70, 74–75, 77, 81 (& note), 88–89, 92, 101
Musical scholarship, 113–114, 118, 120, 122
My Days are Gliding Swiftly By (D. Nelson), 70
My Faith Looks Up to Thee (R. Palmer), 109
My Jesus Purchased Me with Blood (*Mein Jesu kaufte mich mit Blut*, W. Preiss; trans., H. Durnbaugh), 58–59
My Senses are Failing Me (*Wo bleiben meine Sinnen*, A. Mack Jr.; trans., H. Durnbaugh), 31–32
Naas, Johannes (1669–1741), 27, 40–43, 71, 73, 116, 130

Nead, Peter (1796–1877), 15, 63
Neander, Joachim (1650–1680), 13 (& note), 21 (note), 22, 29, 54, 117
Nelson, David (1793–1844), 70
Neue Sammlung (1870), 43, 68, 70–72, 74
NEW BEGINNINGS (R. Brode), 133
Newton, John (1725–1807), 51–52, 70, 83, 93
Nicolai, Philipp (1556–1608), 20 (note), 21–22,
Non-conformity, Non-resistance, Non-swearing 61, 110
North, Frank Mason (1850–1935), 108, 111
Now Breaks This House of Earth in Twain (*Nun bricht der Hütten Haus entzwei*, A. Mack Jr.), 38
Now, Pilgrims, Let Us Go in Peace (S. M. Hoover),
Now Thank We All Our God (*Nun danket alle Gott*, M. Rinkart), 21 (note), 22, 117
Nun bricht der Hütten Haus entzwei (*Now Breaks This House of Earth in Twain*, A. Mack Jr.), 38
NUN DANKET ALLE GOTT (J. Crüger), 21 (note), 22, 117
Nun danket alle Gott (*Now Thank We All Our God*, M. Rinkart), 21 (note), 117
O GOD OF MYSTERY (W. Brumbaugh), 131
O God of Mystery and Might (K. Morse), 131
O Haupt voll Blut und wunden (*O Sacred Head, Sore Wounded*, P. Gerhardt), 21 (note)
O Morning Star, How Fair and Bright (*Wie schön leuchet der Morgenstern*, P. Nicolai), 20 (note)
O Sacred Head, Sore Wounded (*O Haupt voll Blut und wunden*, P. Gerhardt), 21 (note), 117
O! wie ist die Zeit so wichtig (*Oh, How is the Time So Urgent*, J. Stoll; trans., O. Garber), 45–46, 117
Obedience, 14
OBEDIENCE (G. B. Holsinger), 97
Oh, How is the Time So Urgent (*O! wie ist die Zeit so wichtig*, J. Stoll; trans., O. Garber), 45–46, 117
Oh, Who Would Not a Christian Be (S. Kinsey), 79

OLD HUNDREDTH (L. Bourgeois), 114
On the Radiant Threshold (A. C. Wieand), 96, 102, 119
Order of Salvation (rubrics), 29–30, 72, 74
Our Father in Heaven (S. Hale), 134–135
Over-arching theme of Brethren spirituality, 11, 14, 16, 34, 35 (note), 47–48, 53–54, 61, 63, 115
Palmer, Ray (1808–1887), 108–109
Persecution, 23–26
Perseverance, 40
Pfautz, J. E., 58
Pilgrim, pilgrimage, 3, 6, 18–19, 26, 44, 61, 70, 90, 94–95, 104
PINE GLEN (P. Huffaker), 118
PIONEER (N. Fisher), 83, 118–119
Pioneer Brethren musician, 64, 66
Plain manner (unison, unaccompanied, slowly), 15–16, 36, 49
Practical Exercises in Music Reading for Sunday Schools, Day Schools, Institutes and Normals (1908), 91
Praise and worship genre, 126
Praise team, 126
Praise to the Lord, the Almighty (*Lobe den Herren den mächitgen*, J. Neander), 21 (note), 22
Praxis Pietatis Melica (*Practice of Piety in Song*), 21 (note), 23, 120
Prayer is the Soul's Sincere Desire (J. Montgomery), 105–106
Preiss, Johannes (1702–1724), 73
Preiss, Wilhelm (1789–1849), 58, 71, 73
Primitive Christian and Pilgrim, 76–77
Primitive Christianity, 15, 18, 62, 68
Progressive(s), 67–68, 75, 77
Prominent themes, 19, 29, 30 (& note)
QUINTER (G. B. Holsinger), 97
Quinter, James (1816–1888), 12–13, 68–69, 75–75
Responsive readings, 101, 121
Revival (Protracted) meetings, 58, 61, 67–68
Revival songs genre, 58–59, 99

Revivalist piety, 68, 81 (& note), 99

Rinkart, Martin (1586–1649), 21 (note), 22, 117

Rise Up, O Men of God (W. P. Merrill), 109–111

Rist, Johann (1607–1667), 22

Robinson, Paul Minnich (b. 1914), 116, 128–129

Robinson, Robert (1735–1790), 52

Ronk, Albert T. (1886–1972), 11, 111–112

Rosenroth, Christian Knorr von (1636–1689), 117

Round notes, 49 (& note), 81 (& note), 101

Roussakis, Peter E. (b. 1946), 78 (note), 83 (note), 134, 135–6 (& notes)

Royer, Galen B. (1862–1951), 97

Rubrics, 29, 51, 56, 60, 71–72, 74

Rudiments of music, 77, 89

Sanctification, 5

Sanger, Florence Ziegler (b. 1906), 120

Sappington, Roger E. (1929–1989), 44 (note)

Sauer Jr., Christopher (1721–1784), 16, 28, 32–33, 38–40, 73, 116

Sauer Sr., Christopher (1695–1758), 28–29, 33

Sauer, Samuel (1767–1820), 36, 43

Savior of My Soul (*Heiland meiner Seel*, J. Naas; trans., O Garber; & paraphrased, L. Grisso), 42–43, 116, 130

Saxton, John, 57

Schleffer, Johann (1624–1677), 29, 54, 117

Schein, Johann Hermann (1586–1630), 122

Schlosser, Ralph W. (1886–1878), 26 (note)

Schmolck, Benjamin (1672–1737), 114, 117

Schwedler, Johann C. (1672–1730), 117

Schwarzenau, 6, 23, 27

Sectarianism, 61

Sell, James A. (1845–1948), 96

Separation from the world, 61

Service music and worship aids, 101–102, 116, 121, 128, 132

Shacklock, Mrs. C. L., 85

Shape-notes, 64, 75, 77, 89, 92, 101
SHOWALTER (Showalter), 120
Showalter, John Henry (1864–1947), 89, 91–92, 97–98, 113, 120
Simons, Menno (1496–1561), 129
Singing at baptisms, 24–25, 36
Singing at Love Feasts (Communion), 36, 63 (note)
Singing in a plain manner (in unison, unaccompanied, slowly,), 15–16, 36, 49, 64, 84, 127
Singing in parts (harmony), 64, 134
Singing practices 18th century, 15, 18, 28, 35–36, 49
Singing practices 19th century, 15–16, 61, 62–63 (& notes), 64–65, 84
Singing practices 20th century, 97–98, 100–102, 121, 126–127, 134
Singing schools, classes, teachers, 64, 76–77, 84, 91
Smart, Christopher (1722–1771), 131–132
Snowberger, Obed, 39
So Let Our Lips and Lives Express (I. Watts), 54
Social gospel, 99, 109–111, 121
Solingen, 25
Solmization, 64
Song leader (*Vorsänger*), 64, 98
Song services, 97, 98 (note)
Songs of Praises (1906), 91
Songs of Salvation, 121
Spirit, Blowing and Blazing (K. Gibble), 133
Spiritual Magazine (*Ein Geistliches Magazein*), 33
Spirituality, 3, 5–6, 11, 18
Spirituality characteristics and themes 18th century, 3, 5–6, 11, 13–14, 18–19, 33–35, 47
Spirituality characteristics and themes 19th century, 13, 47–51, 53, 61–65, 68–69, 71–72, 74, 79, 81–82, 84–85, 90
Spirituality characteristics and themes 20th century, 93–94, 100, 103–105, 108–109, 115, 123–126, 132
Statler, Ruth B. (1906–2008), 134

Steele, Anne (1716–1778), 70

Stevenson, Robert (1916–2012), 122

Stoffer, Dale R. (b. 1950), 35 (note), 47–49, notes throughout

Stoll, Jakob (1731–1822), 19, 43–46, 60, 73, 117

STRANGERS NO MORE (D. Morningstar), 132–133

Strangers No More (K. Morse), 132

Supplication hymns, 51

Take My Hand and Lead Me, Father (G. A. Flory), 89–90, 102, 112

Tate, Nahum (1652–1715), 52

Tersteegen, Gerhard (1697–1769), 21 (note), 54, 56

The 'Blue' Book, 101

The Brethren Hymnal: A Collection of Psalms, Hymns and Spiritual Song; Suited for Song Service in Christian Worship, for Church Service, Social Meetings and Sunday School (1901), 87, 89, 92–98, 102

The Brethren Hymnal (1951), 38–39, 46, 78, 83, 89, 99, 102, 115–122, 125

The Brethren Hymnody with Tunes, for the Sanctuary, Prayer Meeting, and Home Circle (1884), 66, 81–86, 118

The Brethren Songbook (1974, 1979), 125–126

The Brethren's Sunday School Song Book (1894), 88–92, 102

The Brethren's Tune and Hymn Book (1872, 1879), 66, 70, 74–78, 82–84, 92, 118

The Christian's Duty (1791), 49–54, 57, 70, 74

The Kingdom of God (Arnold; trans. C. Winkworth), 15

The 'Old Black Book', 92

The Pilgrim's Parting Hymn (S. M. Hoover), 94–95

The 'Red' Book, 116

The Vindicator, 78–79

Thou Art a Pilgrim True and Tried (trans., R. W. Schlosser), 26 (& note)

Thou, Poor Pilgrim, Wander'st Here (Becker; trans., J. S. Flory), 37

Thou searchest me (A. Mack Jr.), 32

'Tis Not with Eyes of Flesh We See (O. Garber), 118
Toplady, Augustus (1740–1778), 52, 70, 83
Translations from *Genevan Psalter* into German, 29
Translations of English hymns into German, 71
Translation of German hymns into English, 116, 123, 128
Trine immersion, 25, 28, 55
Tuning fork, 64
Two tracks of Brethren hymnody, 49, 52–53, 72, 93
Überschlag die kost, (*Count the cost*, A. Mack Sr.), 23, 24 (& note), 28
Virginia Normal School (Bridgewater College), 91
WACHET AUF (P. Nicolai), 20 (note), 21, 117
Wachet auf, ruft uns die Stimme (*Wake, Awake, for Night is Flying*, P. Nicolai), 20 (note), 21, 117
Walter, Johannes (1781–1818), 59
Was hat uns doch bewogen (*What is It That Has Led Us*, J. Danner; trans., O. Garber), 55–56
Watts, Isaac (1674–1748), 51, 53–54, 69–70, 79, 83, 93, 104, 112, 121
Wayland, John Walter (1872–1962), 93, 95–97, 102–104
We are People of God's Peace (M. Simons), 129
We bring this person who wishes to be baptized (*Die sen Täufling wir*), 55
Weissel, George (1590–1635), 117
Wenger, Marion (b. 1932), 130
Wesley, Charles (1707–1788), 51, 69, 79, 83, 93, 104, 121
Wesley, John (1703–1791), 107
Wesley, Samuel Sebastian (1810–1876), 114
What is It That Has Led Us (*Was hat uns doch bewogen*, J. Danner; trans., O. Garber), 55–56
What poor, despised company, 70
When the Winds of Misfortune Roar (A. Mack Jr.; trans., S. Heckman), 33, 84
Where Cross the Crowded Ways of Life (F. M. North), 111
Where is this Stupendous Stranger? (C. Smart), 131–132

Whitefield, George (1714–1770), 121
Whittier, John Greenleaf (1807–1892), 121
Wie schön leuchet der Morgenstern (*O Morning Star, How Fair and Bright*, P. Nicolai), 20 (note),
Wieand, Albert Cassel (1871–1954), 96, 100, 102, 119
Williams, William (1717–1791), 52, 58
Wine, Mary Stoner (1885–1959), 103
Winkworth, Catherine (1827–1878), 15
Wittenberg Gesang-Buch (1535), 120
Wo bleiben meine Sinnen (*My Senses are Failing Me*, A. Mack Jr.; trans., H. Durnbaugh), 31–32
World peace and brotherhood, 109–111, 115
Worldlyism, 115
Worship aids, 101–102, 116, 121, 128, 132
Worship practices 18th century, 15, 18–19, 28, 35–36, 46
Worship practices, 19th century, 15, 61, 62–63 (& notes), 64–65
Worship practices, 20th century, 15, 101–102, 116, 121, 126, 128, 132
Yoder, Charles Francis (1873–1955), 100
Youth sing (OGBB), 134
Ziegler, Edward K. (1903–1989), 122

THE AUTHOR'S BIOGRAPHY

Peter Ellwood Roussakis

Born: October 16, 1946, Bridgeport, Connecticut; Ordained: Ashland Theological Seminary, April 23, 1978.

Married: Phyllis Ann Berkshire, October 31, 1970; Two Sons, Alex (b. 1975), Aaron (b. 1976); Seven Grandchildren.

Professional: Senior Pastor, First Brethren Church, Burlington, Indiana (2000–2012); Charles Wesley Professor of Sacred Music, Emeritus, Graduate Theological Foundation, Mishawaka, Indiana (1999–2011); Senior Pastor and Minister of Music for American Baptist Churches of New Hampshire (1986–1999); Assistant Professor of Church Music, Southwestern University, Georgetown, Texas (1980–86); Adjunct Lecturer in Church Music, Ashland Theological Seminary (1977–80); Minister of Music in Kentucky and Ohio (1971–1980); Elementary School Teacher, Trumbull, Connecticut, (1968–1971).

Denominational: Lecturer on Brethren Hymnody for the Fifth Brethren World Assembly, July 11–14, 2013; Joint Worship Committee, Conference Choir Director and Hymnology Lecturer for the 300th Anniversary Conference of the Brethren in Richmond, Virginia, July 2008; Ministerial Examining Board, Executive Board, and Moderator for the Indiana District of The Brethren Church; Song Leader and Pianist, Indiana and Ohio District Conferences of The Brethren Church; Chair of the Worship Committee of The Brethren Church; Worship Leader, Song Leader and Pianist for General Conferences of The Brethren Church.

Educational: BS, MS, Southern Connecticut State University; Master of Church Music, The Southern Baptist Theological Seminary; Royal School of Church Music; Graduate Studies, Ohio University, Ashland Theological Seminary, Harvard University; Master of Sacred Theology, Boston University

School of Theology; Doctor of Ministry, Austin Presbyterian Theological Seminary; Doctor of Philosophy, Graduate Theological Foundation.

Literary: Numerous Articles, Books, Sermons, Compositions: "Brethren Hymnody," *Proceedings of the Fifth Brethren World Assembly July 11–14, 2013*, The Brethren Encyclopedia Inc., 2015; *Feeding the Sheep: Anthology of Manuscript Sermons* (Forthcoming); *John Cook Ewing (1849–1937): Pioneer Brethren Musician, Teacher and Composer* with William Beery, Meetinghouse Press, 2010; "Be Thou My Vision," Piano Solo, Adapted from 'Gymnopedie No. 1' by Erik Satie, with Lenny Seidel, *The Church Pianist* (Vol. 26, No. 1, Sept./Oct. 2009), Lorenz Publishing Company; "Counting the Cost," *The Brethren Evangelist* (Vol. 130, No. 3, May/June 2008); "The Jewish Setting of the Lord's Prayer," *Foundation Theology 2008: Essays for Ministry Professionals,* The Victoria Press, 2008; *United in Prayer: Understanding and Praying the Lord's Prayer,* Meetinghouse Press, 2007; "Praying the Lord's Prayer as Confessing Faith," *Foundation Theology 2006: Essays for Ministry Professionals*, Graduate Theological Foundation, 2006; "Forward" to *The Evangelical Doctrines of Charles Wesley's Hymns* by J. Ernest Rattenbury, Reissued by Meetinghouse Press, 2006, Originally Published by Epworth Press, 1941; *Classic Worship: With Brethren in Mind*, Meetinghouse Press, 2005; *Confessing the Compendium: Praying the Lord's Prayer as Confessing Faith*, PhD Dissertation (1998), Meetinghouse Press, 2005; "Count Well the Cost," Adaptation of Hymn Text by Alexander Mack, Sr. (1679–1735), Leader of the German Baptist Brethren, Adaptation & Setting (Tune: MILAN) Copyright 2005, Meetinghouse Press; "Waldo Selden Pratt (1857–1939): Church Music and the Hartford Connection," *Foundation Theology 2004: Essays for Ministry Professionals*, Graduate Theological Foundation, 2004; "Hymn Singing as Sung Word," *Foundation Theology 2002: Essays for Ministry Professionals*, Graduate

Theological Foundation, 2002; "Introduction" to *Music in Worship: The Use of Music in the Church Service* by Joseph N. Ashton, Wyndham Hall Press, 2001, Originally Published by Pilgrim Press, 1943; Hymn Tune: DEVOTION 65.65.D, set to hymn text "Our Father in Heaven" by Sarah J. Hale (1788–1879), Tune & Setting Copyright 1997; "The Significance of Music in Worship," *Journal of the American Academy of Ministry*, June 1993; "Integrity of Conscience," *Pulpit Digest*, May/June 1993; "The Church Choir," *Leadership in Church Music*, May/June 1992; "Portrait of a Musician: John Cook Ewing (1849–1937)," *The Brethren Evangelist*, December 1984; "Using Analogical Imagination: Interpreting Another's Hymn," *Austin Seminary Bulletin*, April 1983; "Introducing the Conference Worship Committee," *The Brethren Evangelist*, July 1979; "The Music Ministry," *The Brethren Evangelist*, August 23, 1975; "The Multiplied Ministry," *The Brethren Evangelist*, November 30, 1974; "Foundational Hymn Talks" (Series of Articles on Congregational Song), *The Brethren Evangelist*, August 24, 1974, September 7, 1974, October 5, 1974, October 19, 1974; "Foundations of Brethren Hymnody," *The Brethren Evangelist*, June 1973.

ENDORSEMENT for *Classic Worship: With Brethren in Mind*

Dr. Roussakis brings a sharp awareness to the importance of worship by the Book; and from that Bible-based foundation he calls us to review our worship practices. It is an impassioned study of worship, Biblically informed and congregationally designed; a good, well ordered challenge to worship leaders and pastors. It deserves a reading by all who desire to be faithful to scripture in worship. *Dr. Charles R. Munson, Professor of Practical Theology Emeritus (Deceased), Ashland Theological Seminary, Ashland, Ohio.*

REVIEW for *United in Prayer: Understanding and Praying the Lord's Prayer*

Peter Roussakis (Ph.D., Graduate Theological Foundation), is a Brethren Pastor and professor in Indiana. He opens his treatment of the Lord's Prayer with an overview of it and description of its Jewish setting. He devotes substantial attention to God's name and what it means to enter and increase in God's kingdom. Two chapters are given to imagining the kingdom of glory and how a Christian's death means passing from the kingdom of grace to the kingdom of glory. Exposition follows on depending on God for provision, seeking forgiveness and forgiving others, praying for leniency and deliverance, and praising God. Concluding chapters offer helps on teaching the prayer to children and the value of using it in corporate and individual worship. There are questions for reflection and discussion, while an extensive bibliography shows the breadth of the author's reading. Roussakis draws heavily from older, classic writers (Luther, Watson, Calvin, and Wesley), but he does not ignore contemporary authors. The broad research and orderly pastoral presentation of *United in Prayer* give it a solid, workmanlike feel. ... [It offers] growing disciples another look at aspects of Christian spirituality that should become, in the best sense, habitual ("customary, steady"). *Dr. Jerry R. Flora, Professor Emeritus of Theology and Spiritual Formation (Retired), Ashland Theological Journal Volume XLI, 2009, 180–181.*

www.ingramcontent.com/pod-product-compliance
Lightning Source LLC
Chambersburg PA
CBHW071434160426
43195CB00013B/1900